# DISCOVERING THE POWER OF
# GOD IN YOU

*Overcoming Adversity and Thriving in Your Gifts*

## DR. KAZUMBA CHARLES

WESTBOW
PRESS®
A DIVISION OF THOMAS NELSON
& ZONDERVAN

Copyright © 2017 Dr. Kazumba Charles.

All rights reserved. No part of this book may be used or reproduced by any means, graphic, electronic, or mechanical, including photocopying, recording, taping or by any information storage retrieval system without the written permission of the author except in the case of brief quotations embodied in critical articles and reviews.

Scripture quotations marked HCSB®, are taken from the Holman Christian Standard Bible®, Copyright © 1999, 2000, 2002, 2003, 2009 by Holman Bible Publishers. Used by permission. HCSB® is a federally registered trademark of Holman Bible Publishers

The Holy Bible, English Standard Version® (ESV®)
Copyright © 2001 by Crossway,
a publishing ministry of Good News Publishers.
All rights reserved.
ESV Text Edition: 2016

Scripture taken from the New King James Version®. Copyright © 1982 by Thomas Nelson. Used by permission. All rights reserved.

Scripture quotations marked (NIV) are taken from the Holy Bible, New International Version®, NIV®. Copyright © 1973, 1978, 1984, 2011 by Biblica, Inc.™ Used by permission of Zondervan. All rights reserved worldwide. www.zondervan.com The "NIV" and "New International Version" are trademarks registered in the United States Patent and Trademark Office by Biblica, Inc.™

Scripture taken from the Holy Bible: International Standard Version® Release 2.0. Copyright © 1996-2013 by the ISV Foundation. Used by permission of Davidson Press, LLC. ALL RIGHTS RESERVED INTERNATIONALLY.

Scripture quotations taken from the New American Standard Bible® (NASB),
Copyright © 1960, 1962, 1963, 1968, 1971, 1972, 1973,
1975, 1977, 1995 by The Lockman Foundation
Used by permission. www.Lockman.org

Scripture quotations are taken from the Holy Bible, New Living Translation, copyright ©1996, 2004, 2007, 2013, 2015 by Tyndale House Foundation. Used by permission of Tyndale House Publishers, Inc., Carol Stream, Illinois 60188. All rights reserved.

WestBow Press books may be ordered through booksellers or by contacting:

WestBow Press
A Division of Thomas Nelson & Zondervan
1663 Liberty Drive
Bloomington, IN 47403
www.westbowpress.com
1 (866) 928-1240

Because of the dynamic nature of the Internet, any web addresses or links contained in this book may have changed since publication and may no longer be valid. The views expressed in this work are solely those of the author and do not necessarily reflect the views of the publisher, and the publisher hereby disclaims any responsibility for them.

Any people depicted in stock imagery provided by Thinkstock are models, and such images are being used for illustrative purposes only. Certain stock imagery © Thinkstock.

ISBN: 978-1-5127-8756-6 (sc)
ISBN: 978-1-5127-8755-9 (hc)
ISBN: 978-1-5127-8757-3 (e)

Library of Congress Control Number: 2017907845

Print information available on the last page.

WestBow Press rev. date: 05/19/2017

*THIS BOOK WILL HELP YOU BREAK OUT OF ORDINARY STATUS QUO CHRISTIANITY AND BOLDLY FULFILL THE EXTRAORDINARY CALL OF GOD ON YOUR LIFE. NOW IS YOUR TIME TO WAKE UP FROM YOUR SLUMBER AND FUNCTION IN THE POWER OF THE KINGDOM OF GOD!*

# CONTENTS

| | | |
|---|---|---|
| Foreword | | ix |
| Acknowledgments | | xiii |
| Introduction | | xv |
| Chapter 1 | GOD IS WAITING ON YOU | 1 |
| Chapter 2 | WHEN GOD REIGNS IN YOU | 26 |
| Chapter 3 | DISCOVERING THE POWER OF GOD IN YOU | 50 |
| Chapter 4 | THE POWER OF JESUS' NAME | 79 |
| Chapter 5 | FUNCTIONING IN THE POWER OF YOUR GIFTS | 105 |
| Chapter 6 | AWAKENING THE FIRE OF GOD WITHIN YOU | 129 |
| Chapter 7 | OBSTACLES COME BEFORE DESTINY | 152 |
| Chapter 8 | HEARING THE VOICE OF GOD IN A CRISIS | 172 |
| Chapter 9 | I AM WHO GOD SAYS I AM | 193 |
| Chapter 10 | IT'S TIME TO RISE UP | 213 |
| Conclusion | | 233 |
| 30 Inspirational Quotes to Feed Your Spirit | | 237 |
| About the Author | | 241 |

# FOREWORD

In Hebrew there is no word for *coincidence*. I truly believe the hand of God was on me that day, guiding that "chance" meeting with Kazumba Charles. While shopping I needed help with a heavy item. Looking up, I noticed Charles and asked for his assistance. There was something different about him. He had a big smile on his face; his eyes were kind, and his demeanor was humble. I was curious about this unique man who radiated joy and peace. He stayed with me, insisting on helping me load my cumbersome item. We chatted about various things as we waited in line, and the topic rolled around to Jesus and the Jewishness of Jesus. Wow! A man of God in the middle of Princess Auto in Saskatoon, Saskatchewan, Canada. As we headed outside to load my purchase, Charles spoke about Yeshua with such love, passion, and intimacy that my heart leapt—finally someone who had the passion and zeal for the things of God my husband and I did. We were tired of big-box religion, tired of the latest, greatest craze in Christianity, tired of the same old thing week after week, having our ears tickled with kind, nice words but no meat or substance from the depth of God and His Holy Word. When I found out Charles was studying for his master's degree in theology, I knew he was dedicated to understanding the fullness of Yahweh.

It has been an absolute joy to see this mighty man of God grow, expanding the realm of his knowledge and understanding and fulfilling the dream the Lord birthed in Charles to achieve his doctorate of theology. That dream was achieved by great sacrifices, not only by Charles himself but also by his wife, Glory, and their three children. Many times over the years the whole family has prayed and fasted, seeking the face of God and asking and receiving the breakthroughs and answers they desired in a variety of situations. God is faithful. Now Dr. Kazumba has taken that intimate relationship he has with his heavenly Father and shared his godly knowledge, wisdom, and discernment with the rest of the world. Dr. Charles uses plain, simple terms and language everyone can understand, whether one is a believer in Jesus the Messiah or not.

Through the years I have seen Charles rise up, taking his position as a watchman on the wall, sounding the alarm, telling people we must repent and get all things right with our Lord and creator Elohim. Time is of the essence; it is with great urgency that he declares this message around the world through all avenues, means, and measures that have been made available to him. Dr. Charles has been faithful to God in all areas of his life, and I have seen firsthand how God has opened doors and windows of opportunity, quickly and suddenly, that would seem impossible for the average person to attain in a lifetime. That is the blessing and favor of Adonai at work. That is the just reward for a faithful servant.

The way God has knit our lives, our paths, and our ministries together has been a joy to behold. Charles has gently and lovingly tipped over some sacred cows that were deeply imbedded in my belief system to engage and challenge me to delve into the real truth of God. At times he has used ancient texts, translations, and manuscripts to bring clarity to my heart and mind, thus causing my love for God and His Holy Word to grow, increasing my hunger for His truth and righteousness, and encouraging me never to stop growing in the things of God. It has been an honor and privilege to be a small part of his life, his family, his ministry (Christ Passion

Evangelistic Ministries), and his TV program (*Kingdom Insights*). It is refreshing to walk with a man of God who is not swayed by man's opinions or popular Christian trends, cannot be lured by fame, fortune, or success, and is not bound by denominational doctrines and theologies or the creeds of man but stays true to the Holy Word of God and the timeless teachings of Jesus Messiah. Dr. Charles keeps the language and the lessons plain, simple, and to the point so everyone and anyone around the world, from Christian to atheist to agnostic, from the most learned to the most simple, can understand, appreciate, and apply his teachings.

Andy and Irena Broadfoot
Chaplains, God Speed Ministry
Watrous, Saskatchewan, Canada

# ACKNOWLEDGMENTS

I would like to thank my Lord and Savior Jesus Christ for saving my life and preserving it to bring glory and honor to His name. Everything I do and have done in the past years for the kingdom of God is all because of God's mercy, grace, and anointing that He has graciously poured out on me. Without Jesus Christ and the power of the Holy Spirit, I am nothing. Thank You, Lord Jesus, for Your amazing grace and love for me and my family. I am humbled by Your extravagant love and for calling me to serve in Your kingdom at such a time as this. As long as You are with me, Lord, I will go wherever You send me and proclaim Your good news and make Your name known as You have made Yourself known to me.

I thank my partner and coworker in ministry, my wife, Glory Kazumba, who has been such a great support and pillar in my life, and our precious and wonderful children, Louriana, Briona, and Joshua McCharles. I am also indebted to my mother, Juliet Kabwe Kazumba, who is my spiritual hero and inspiration. Thanks also to Dr. David Pierce and his precious wife, Joyce Pierce. You both invested everything you could in my life and family just to see us serve God effectively and powerfully. You saw the grace of God, the gift of God, and the call of God on my life. Consequently, you invested your time to cultivate, train, and develop us through the Word of God to be what we are today in the kingdom of God—disciples and followers of Jesus Christ. And a big thank-you to all our friends and partners of Christ Passion Evangelistic Ministries around the world who have graciously supported and prayed for me, my family, and the ministry God has entrusted to us. May the Lord bless you and continuously watch over you.

I also wish to acknowledge Bishop Andrew Bills, director and founder of the Holy Spirit Broadcasting Network in Santa Ana, California, and Irena and Andy Broadfoot of Watrous, Saskatchewan, Canada. Bishop Bills, you saw the gifts and anointing of God on my life and ministry and graciously brought me onto HSBN TV and Radio so the world could be impacted by the Word of God. Thank you so much for your kingdom heart and spirit. Irena and Andy Broadfoot, you have faithfully supported our ministry year in and year out and stood with us in prayer and encouraged us to go for God and win souls for Jesus Christ. May the Lord bless you and continue to watch over you. Finally, I would like to say thank you to my big brother and partner in ministry, Garett Balan. Thank you for all your love and financial and prayer support. May the Lord continue to bless you.

# INTRODUCTION

In today's world, it is suicidal for us as Christians to try to live the Christian life without the power and presence of God operating in our hearts and being revealed in our lifestyles. Furthermore, it is detrimental to live life without knowing who we are in Christ, what we have in Him, and why God created us. Additionally, living life without knowing the power we have in Christ and what we could do with that power leads to a frustrating, confusing, unfruitful, and unfulfilled life. We can have creative ideas, exciting gifts, a great church, and a terrific plan to transform the world. However, if we are not walking in the power of the kingdom of God, our great ideas will never materialize into anything tangible. Too often we have wonderful plans for what we will do or be for God, but we lack the power to carry out those plans. We need to understand that no spiritual plan or work can be fulfilled without the tangible power of the kingdom of God at work.

God's plans, ways, and thoughts are different from ours. His plans involve bringing to earth the reality of His kingdom as it exists in heaven. Through you and me, as the body of Christ, the reality of the kingdom of God is revealed to the world. *No person can advance the kingdom of God alone or live a kingdom lifestyle without the presence of God.* We are not talking about feelings here—we are talking about the real and tangible anointing and power of God. His power manifests itself through healing, deliverance, and transformation and empowers people with kingdom abilities to bring the government of the kingdom of God into the hearts of people. With everything evil going on in our world, a good plan or sermon alone will not bring change to the nations. This will occur only when God's people *discover*—or rediscover—and *awaken* the power of the kingdom of God that is silently sleeping inside them.

## Why Do We Need to Discover the Power of God within Us?

Without the power of the kingdom of God working in and through us, it is *impossible* to

- Advance the kingdom of God here on earth
- Overcome the schemes of the kingdom of darkness
- Rescue or set free those who are still in bondage to the forces of darkness
- Influence people for Jesus Christ with the good news of the kingdom
- Demonstrate to the nations the true character and nature of God and His kingdom
- Unleash the rule and reign of God in dark places
- Walk and work in unity with other believers in Christ as one body
- Walk in love, forgiveness, and peace with other people
- Walk in authority, power, and dominion over the forces of darkness
- Heal the sick and win souls for the kingdom of God
- Live a fruitful and prosperous life in Christ
- Win our spiritual battles in life and live victoriously

Too many people are living under enemy oppression. It is time for God's people to rise up in the power and authority of God and snatch these people away from the enemy's influence. We need the manifest power of God at work in us if we are to bring freedom, life, salvation, and revival fire to the nations. The goal of this book is to awaken the fire of God, the gifts of God, and the power of God in all believers in Christ and help them discover how to function and walk in the power of the kingdom of God. Furthermore, through this book readers who belong to God will learn how to exercise God's authority both inside and outside the church. God is calling the church, His people, to function within and outside the local church to bring the goodness of His domain to the broken. We are not called to hide our gifts or talents and just sit in church services Sunday after Sunday without doing anything for the kingdom of God. We are called both individually and corporately to do great works for the kingdom of God. But the truth is, we cannot do great things for God by standing still and doing nothing. We all must do what God is calling us to do in the power and authority God has given each of us.

You have a measure of authority and power that God has graciously made available to you through the gifts He has invested in you. Now it is time for you to activate those gifts and begin walking in their power so God can work through you to bring healing, restoration, deliverance, and life to those around you. As you *discover* and *awaken* the power of the kingdom of God in you, God will use you mightily, and you will bring meaning and fulfillment to your life in Christ.

This book will set you on fire for God and empower you to live your life under the power and anointing of God. It is time to win your battles and use your gifts to bring the rule and reign of the kingdom of God to the hearts of the brokenhearted. You have within you what it takes to do extraordinary works of God. You need only to reactivate the power of God—and that is what this book will provoke you to do. Through this book you will also discover that complaining about the circumstances you are facing does not help change that situation. Difficult life situations will change only when you begin to rise up in faith and in the power of the Word of God.

My prayer is that this book will transform your spiritual life and that God will use it to motivate, inspire, empower, and encourage you to rise up in His power and use your gifts to do exploits for the kingdom of God. The goal of this book is to give you deeper kingdom insight into who you are and what you have in Christ and to help you discover the Holy Spirit power you have as a born-again Christian. *Inside you resides the dynamic power and authority of God through the gifts God has put within you. If you rise up and use those gifts to the glory and honor of God, then you will reign and rule with God and live a fruitful, meaningful, satisfying, victorious, and overcoming life here on earth.*

# Chapter 1

# GOD IS WAITING ON YOU

Functioning in the Power of His Spirit

The Angel of the LORD came, and He sat under the oak that was in Ophrah, which belonged to Joash, the Abiezrite. His son Gideon was threshing wheat in the wine vat to hide it from the Midianites. Then the Angel of the LORD appeared to him and said: "The LORD is with you, mighty warrior." Gideon said to Him, "Please Sir, if the LORD is with us, why has all this happened? And where are all His wonders that our fathers told us about? They said, 'Hasn't the LORD brought us out of Egypt?' But now the LORD has abandoned us and handed us over to Midian." The LORD turned to him and said, "Go in the strength you have and deliver Israel from the power of Midian. Am I not sending you?" (Judges 6:11–14 HCSB)

*Dr. Kazumba Charles*

## Rise Up through the Strength of God within You

As we can see in the above passage, Gideon was waiting for God to come to rescue Israel from their enemies, the Midianites, who had terrorized them for some time. Gideon was scared and accused God of abandoning His people and handing them over to their enemies. Gideon was so focused on the magnitude of the problem at hand and the power of the enemy that he felt powerless and hopeless. He obviously looked at himself as a limited person who could do nothing about the situation. He was looking for God to act.

The significant issue here is that Gideon did not know God saw him as a mighty warrior of God full of His strength—as a man capable of delivering Israel from its enemies. So often we sit and complain about our life circumstances and look for people who will help us find deliverance or who will fight for us so we can turn our situations around. Certainly, there is nothing wrong with seeking help from others, but we need to remember that while others can give us wisdom, training, or ideas, no person can fight our battles for us. We must arise in the strength and power of God within us, and we must fight our own battles.

God is waiting for you to rise up and spiritually fight the enemy who has terrorized your life, family, marriage, or church. You may feel powerless, but you are a mighty person of valor and full of God's power. Stop complaining about your situation or focusing on how bad your troubles are. Through God, you can turn things around in your life this very moment. God has not abandoned you, and He is not the cause of your troubles—Satan is. You may feel as though you are nothing—that you are overpowered by your troubles in life. However, according to God you are a mighty, strong, powerful, and victorious warrior who just needs to arise in faith, believe the Word of God, and act on His promises. He has promised He will go with you and will never fail you or forsake you (Deuteronomy 31:6). Whatever you may be going through right now, you need to look to God, be strong and courageous in Him, and do not fear, for God will fight through you and give you victory.

Turn to the Word of God and stand on what it says. The Word of God is a great, powerful, inspirational, life-changing pillar that helps us build sustainable and victorious lives. It contains the words of life and the very breath of God. It can change the course of our lives forever if we believe it and implement its teachings. The Word is our manual not only for how we can build our lives but also for how we can live for God's glory and in His power here on the earth and serve His kingdom most effectively.

Furthermore, the Bible is full of life-changing accounts of godly people who powerfully functioned in their gifts and kingdom authority. They brought spiritual revolution and changed their communities—and they even changed places beyond their own borders. These people of God refused to allow the enemy to bully, intimidate, manipulate, or destroy their God-given visions and dedication to God. These Bible heroes responded to difficult situations by believing God and standing firm on His Word and His character; they did not allow their faith in the Lord, Yahweh, to be shaken. Consequently, they acted on the Word of God and fulfilled God's call on their lives. And God was faithful in providing protection and helping them defeat their enemies.

Perhaps the most interesting thing about these Bible heroes is that they did not wait for someone else to act on their behalf to bring about needed change that would bring glory and honor to Yahweh's name. They personally took responsibility by doing something about the situations they faced.

When the walls of Jerusalem were broken down, Nehemiah did not just talk about rebuilding them or wait for someone else to do so. He took full responsibility and acted, assembling his people to rebuild the broken walls despite opposition from their enemy. How about the young David? The entire army of Israel was too afraid to confront the giant Goliath. For forty days Israel's army stood still in fear as Goliath taunted them. But when David heard Goliath's taunting, he rose up, confronted Goliath, and defeated him. The army of Israel had the training and weapons David lacked, but their fear had prevented them from putting their military training into action.

And finally, think about Daniel, Shadrach, Meshach, and Abednego. These powerful men of God did not just know God and know His Word—they believed God and believed His Word. Consequently, they refused to acknowledge any other so-called god even in the face of imminent danger or death. When it mattered most to demonstrate their true love and loyalty to Yahweh, the God of Israel, these men stood their ground and refused to honor the foreign gods of the Babylonian king Nebuchadnezzar. This illustrated their obedience, love, faith, and loyalty to God Almighty. They set a great example of what it means to love and serve the only true God without wavering even in the face of death. And in the end, God responded by extending His hand of protection, proving that Yahweh alone is the mighty and living God.

The world is facing countless spiritual and social problems today, but many Christians seem to be waiting for someone else to do something instead of rising up in the power of God and serving as the catalyst of change, healing, and restoration to both the body of Christ and their nations. It is time to overcome our fears and let God arise in us and demonstrate His love, mercy, grace, and power through us.

*Discovering the Power of God in You*

I strongly believe that today God is looking for men and women of substance, purpose, and faith—people who are fearless and determined. He is looking for men and women who believe God's Word—people who can function in the power of the gifts He has placed in them, and people who are willing to take God at His word and trust Him even in the face of danger to bring the gospel of His kingdom to those who are perishing. While many of us are waiting on God or some "qualified" few to change the world, God is waiting on us to act on His Word and go forth in His power to do what He has ordained us all to do: announce His kingdom's arrival here on the earth, heal the sick, mend the brokenhearted, and proclaim the year of His favor. God is waiting for us to return to Him, to walk in His presence, and to function in the power of His kingdom.

Any situation you may be facing can be fixed or changed by simply responding to the Word of God and allowing God to move in your life. It is important to understand that neither our problems nor the spiritual condition of the world today will change if you and I just sit around and complain about them. But conditions will surely change if we respond to the power of God's Word and earnestly pray. Faith takes action. Faith calls us to pray, because prayer is so powerful that it can change any life situation or condition.

God is waiting for you to be a man or woman of action and not one who just sits dormant and cries about everything going wrong in your life. You have a gift, calling, or talent, but you will never fulfill your great potential until you respond to God in faith. You need to step out of your comfort zone by faith and actively use your gift, talent, or calling to bring change in the world. God is waiting on you to move. When you do, He will move through you to do what He intends to do in the world. Stop looking at others to do something. Look at yourself and allow God to empower and anoint you for such a time as this.

*Dr. Kazumba Charles*

## What and Whom Are You Waiting For?

If you are waiting on someone to bring your dream to fulfillment or someone to develop your gifts or talents, you will be waiting a long time! Yes, we need people to help us and guide us to do what God has called us to do and to be what God wants us to be. However, it is up to us to first recognize the gifts God has deposited in us and take a step forward to nurture them, develop them, and walk in them. Every tool you need to develop your life, win your spiritual battles, and fulfill God's call on your life has been deposited inside you by God. Indeed, God Himself is your protection, victory, salvation, and strength, so there is no need to fear anything. Through this book you will learn how you can break away from the power of fear and break into your God-given destiny. Furthermore, you will learn how you can fulfill God's will in your life and live in the fullness of His power and glory.

God is waiting on each of us to function in the power and ability He has deposited in us through the Holy Spirit and His spiritual gifts so we can demonstrate the goodness of His kingdom. God doesn't give us gifts so we can feel good or important but so we can function in them and realize the government of God's kingdom here on earth.

*The Power of Fear and Negativity*

Many people have allowed life's circumstances to "kill" or freeze out their God-given gifts. For others, fear, especially fear of people, has silenced or paralyzed their gifts. Don't let that happen to you. This is your time to fan into flames the gifts of God within you. As you read this book, your gifts, talents, and passion will be revived by the power of the Word of God so you can be and do what God designed you to be and do for His kingdom. You are not called to be a photocopy of others and do exactly what they are doing. God created you in a unique way, with a distinctive anointing and special gifts in you that you can use to benefit the entire kingdom of God. Yes, you can get inspiration and motivation from others, but you are not called to imitate them. God created you unique for a specific job for His kingdom. For this reason, you should never feel as if you are less important than others—your talents and gifts are crucial to the kingdom of God.

If negative words have destroyed your confidence and ability to function in the power of your gifts, the Spirit of God will change that as you allow God's Word to penetrate your heart. By the time you finish reading this book, I strongly believe the Spirit of the living God will have brought you life, boldness, passion, and determination and revived your vision to serve Him and do exploits for His kingdom. God is waiting on you to function and to display His power, goodness, mercy, grace, love, forgiveness, and life to every person you encounter.

The enemy may have lied to you, accusing you of being useless and not gifted enough to do anything for the kingdom of God. However, through this book you will discover your kingdom power and how to walk in it to bring glory and honor to God and to serve in the body of Christ. In the kingdom of God, everyone is useful. God has put His kingdom power in all believers so we can demonstrate His dominion over the kingdom of darkness and reflect the characteristics of the kingdom of God. God has gifted His people, but many are too timid to use their gifts because they lack fire and passion. The church is suffering and the world is hurting because so many of God's people are afraid to function in the power of the kingdom of God. We need to rediscover and reignite the Holy Spirit power of the kingdom that resides in us if we are to bring transformation into the world.

*Dr. Kazumba Charles*

*Waiting Is Not an Option*

Many people aspire to do great things in life and desire to be used by God, but they *wait on God* to do something miraculous in their life while they sit and do nothing. Just because you want something from God does not mean God will automatically give it to you or do it for you. And just because God has promised to do something for you or for a nation does not mean He will do it without the active involvement of people. God still works with and through people, which means people must be actively involved in every process. God's work is accomplished through prayer and action-faith. God is not a dictator. He will never impose His blessings or will on anyone. His desire for each of us is that we willingly choose to allow Him to move in our life by responding to His Word. If you want God to use you mightily or bring healing or restoration into your life, you must understand this: God will not do so without your involvement or participation. Yes, He could do everything without man's involvement or participation. After all, He is God, the creator of the earth. He created the earth without man's involvement. But God delights in working with His creation (human beings) to bring glory and honor to His name and to display His majestic power over the kingdom of darkness and all its agents.

God wants to bring healing, change, transformation, revival, and blessings to the world and to you and me so we can bring honor and glory to His awesome name. But we need to understand clearly that He will not bring these things into reality if we don't pray and do something practical on our part. For every stronghold in our lives, cities, and nations to be broken, we need to pray. We also need to walk out our prayers. What does this mean? It means we can't simply pray, "God change our city, win souls in this city, and bring revival to our nation," without going out to share the gospel of Jesus Christ with the people in our city and nation. Praying is powerful and does great wonders, but we also need to learn to exercise our faith after we have prayed and go out in the power of the Holy Spirit and do the work of God. There is always great fruit when believers in Christ step out in faith and pray to God and do His work without fear. As we pray for souls and for God's intervention in the problems and troubles the world is facing today, we also need to be active in sharing the powerful gospel of Christ with all humanity. Prayer destroys the works of Satan and ties him down. However, it is up to us to go forth in faith and plunder his house by rescuing lost souls, healing the sick, mending the brokenhearted with the Word of God, and proclaiming the year of the Lord's favor upon His people.

God works through people, and He wants to work through us to bring His rule into this world. Therefore, He empowers us with His Spirit and His Word. It is important to understand that without the power of the Holy Spirit working in us, it is impossible not only to walk in love but also to defeat the plans of the Evil One that are at work against us. In Mark 3:27 Jesus made it clear: "No one can enter a strong man's house and rob his possessions unless he first ties up the strong man, then he will rob his house." In other words, before we can forcefully rob Satan, "the strong man" of lost souls or the sick, we need to first tie him down. Otherwise he will overpower us. How do we tie Satan down? We tie him down through the weapons of prayer, praise, worship, and the word of our testimony of the redeeming power and work of the cross. Without these weapons, it is impossible to overcome the spiritual forces of this world.

When we pray and glorify God through praise and worship, Satan is disarmed. In the book of Joshua we see a great example of how God works with and through man to finish the battle He has already won.

> The Lord said to Joshua, "Look, I have handed Jericho, its king, and its fighting men to you. *March around* the city with all the men of war, circling the city one time. Do this for six days. Have seven

> priests carry seven ram's-horn trumpets in front of the ark. But on the seventh day, march around the city seven times, while the priests blow the trumpets. When there is a prolonged blast of the horn and you hear its sound, have all the people give a mighty shout. Then the city wall will collapse, and the people will advance, each man straight ahead."
> (Joshua 6:2–5, emphasis added)

God told Joshua that Jericho, its king, and its fighting men were already delivered into his hands—that is, the enemy was already defeated. So why did He command Joshua and his people to march around the city once a day for six days and then seven times on the seventh day until the priests blew the trumpets and the people gave a mighty shout?

God had already given Joshua the victory, but Joshua needed to go out there and claim it by responding in a practical way to God's unique instruction. At the sound of the trumpets and the shout of the people, the walls of Jericho came crumbling down. If Joshua had decided to just sit without following God's instruction, the walls of Jericho could have not been brought down even though God had already said He had given Joshua and the Israelites the victory.

As Christians, we find victory assured for us in whatever battle we may be fighting because we fight a defeated enemy. Satan, our enemy and the engineer of evil, has been defeated by the power of the blood of Jesus (see Hebrews 2:14–15; Romans 8:37–39; 1 John 3:8). But we cannot just sit in our rocking chair doing nothing because God has given us victory over Satan. Satan has been defeated, but he is constantly on the attack and will continue attacking God's people. We can finish him off and walk in our Christ-given victory through the power of prayer and by the word of our testimony. Our tongue is a weapon, and through it we can pull down all the strongholds simply by declaring the Word of God and by praising and glorifying Him no matter our situation or circumstance in life.

Revelation 12:11 tells us, "They conquered him by the blood of the Lamb and by the word of their testimony, for they did not love their lives in the face of death." Satan was defeated when Jesus, the Lamb of God, shed his blood for our sins. Through the death of Jesus Christ, the penalty for our sins was paid in full, granting us victory over death and over the angel of death himself, Satan. Although we still fight battles every day that Satan brings upon us, the great news is that we don't fight from a position of defeat; we fight from a position of victory and God's strength. We overcome each day by opening our mouth and declaring into the atmosphere that Yahweh is powerful, living, and majestic in all His ways, and there is none more powerful than He. He alone is worthy of our praise and honor. In Him we live, move, and have our being (Acts 17:28), so there is no need to live in fear. We have a great and mighty God on our side.

God has already released into your hands everything you need to be or become in life, but you must be willing to get out of your comfort zone and pursue your calling. Here is what God said to Jeremiah: "I chose you before I formed you in the womb; I set you apart before you were born. I appointed you a prophet to the nations" (Jeremiah 1:5). God appointed Jeremiah as His prophet to bring His word to the nations and kingdoms long before Jeremiah was born. But again, when the right time came, Jeremiah had to step out into his calling and fulfill his mission.

God has given you gifts, talents, and skills; now He is waiting on you to walk in them without fear. Your fear may be holding you back from using the gifts God has placed within you to help the body of Christ and be a channel through which He can touch many lives. Fear has paralyzed and destroyed many Christians' gifts and God's vision for their lives; hence, the body of Christ is unfruitful because the gifts in the body of Christ are either dormant or dead. The church is powerful and forceful when God's people function in their gifts. But too often people struggle to cultivate their gifts simply because they fear the challenges that lie ahead of them. They lack confidence and feel they have inadequate ability, training, or experience to use their gifts to the glory of God. They wait on someone to encourage them or to say, "You can do it!" Certainly, it is great to be encouraged by others, but you must trust God's Word and believe Him beyond any reasonable doubt by stepping out in faith and doing what He has called you to do. You have tremendous potential and ability to do great things in life if only you will trust God without doubting Him.

*Returning to God*

The question for you is this: What or whom are you waiting for to actualize your gifts? If you are waiting on people or God to make them a reality, then you will be waiting for a long time, because God is waiting for you to use what He already has blessed you with to the glory of His name. What are you waiting for? Why aren't you responding to the Word of God and unleashing your gifts and walking into your destiny so God can demonstrate His mighty powers in your life? Are you waiting for someone or for the right moment before you can use your gifts? What do you think must happen before you can function in your calling? Are you waiting on God? Well, God is waiting on you! Isaiah 30:18 tells us, "Therefore the Lord is waiting to show you mercy, and is rising up to show you compassion, for the Lord is a just God. All who wait patiently for Him are happy." God was and has always been waiting for His people to return to Him and repent so He can turn His judgment into compassion and restoration. That means before God can demonstrate His compassion and bring restoration, people must first return to Him. Restoration will never come if people do not repent, turn away from evil, and return to God. God is waiting on you to arise and turn to Him so you can walk in His power.

In 2 Chronicles 7:14 we see the same idea: "If my people, who are called by my name, will humble themselves and pray and seek my face and turn from their wicked ways, then I will hear from heaven, and I will forgive their sin and will heal their land." The people of God needed to do four things before God would hear them from heaven, forgive their sins, and heal their land. They needed to (1) humble themselves by admitting their sins, (2) pray to God, asking for forgiveness, (3) seek His face, and (4) turn away from sinful behavior, or wickedness. For God to hear their prayer and provide for them, the people in Solomon's care had to do something—namely, turn back to Him. God gives choices to humanity and will never force anyone to return to Him. If you need God to do something with your life and turn your life from fruitlessness to fruitfulness … from hopelessness to hope … and from lifelessness to life, you need to return to Him in humility, pray, and seek His presence. First John 1:9 tell us, "If we confess our sins, he is faithful and righteous to forgive us our sins and to cleanse us from all unrighteousness." God is always ready and waiting to show compassion to the humble, lift them up in the power of His glory, and use them mightily to be a blessing on His behalf to the nations.

"Return to me … and I will return to you" (Zechariah 1:3; see also Jeremiah 4:1; Hosea 14:1) is a reassuring principle and key to living a life of breakthroughs and victory here on earth. When we return to God, God returns His presence and protection to us. Furthermore, when God is on our side and we are in His presence, there is nothing we cannot do or be in His kingdom. When we walk faithfully with God and stand on His Word, nothing will block us from living out our destiny and calling in Him. The problem is that we try to live out our destiny without God and depend too much on our own knowledge and wisdom. A godly destiny is fulfilled when we align our life with God, His Word, and His Spirit. It is important to understand that before God can do something with our life, we must first *return* to Him. We must desire to rid our life of those detestable things that prevent Him from doing what He wants to do in us and through us. When we return to God, God will return to us and cause us to live in His presence. It is when we are in God's presence that we begin to see the goodness and greatness of His majestic kingdom.

Returning to God is an act that involves going back to God's original intention for our life and recognizing all that God says He is to His creation. As we return to God, we begin to fulfill our potential and become what God originally designed us to be—fruitful and powerful in this world. God's wonders and greatness begin to show themselves in our life when we draw closer to Him and He comes closer to us. Many people are spiritually powerless, feeble, fearful, lost, and empty because they are trying to live life without the presence and power of God. We are strong, spiritually stable, and powerful in life only when God's presence is in us and with us. For God to do what He wants to do in the earth today, we, the people of His pasture, must first humble ourselves and turn away from the influence of the world that has consumed and contaminated our godly vessels. We must not only pray about our needs but also continually seek and desire His presence.

*Time for Action*

God is waiting for the church (the people) to wake up from their slumber and function in the power of His Holy Spirit so the world can see the true character and nature of His kingdom. It is not enough just to hear or know the Word of God—we must act on it. We are called to function in the power of God by doing His Word and will. When will we move from talking to action, from praying for a move of God to being a person through whom God can move, and from seeking God's blessings to being a blessing to others?

God is waiting for you. He wants to use you to touch many lives. Stop looking for someone else; God wants to manifest His glory through *you*. You just need to get your life in order and allow God to be God in your life, not limiting Him in any way. Don't doubt God. Believe Him and His Word.

Moses said to God, "What if they will not believe me or listen to what I say?" The Lord responded by asking him a question: "What is in your hand?" (Exodus 4:1–2). God is asking us that same question this very moment: "What is in your hand?" What gift or talent or skill has God blessed you with? Use it and see God multiply it and bless you even more. Don't spend years looking for what you don't have; use what you currently have to get what you don't have. When you use what is already in your hand, it will be used by God to open other doors in your life. Those doors will lead you to God's original plan for your life. That is how our God works. Don't limit or despise the gift or talent within you, and don't envy someone else's gift or talent. Yours is designed to help you accomplish what God has designed you to do. Believe God and step out in faith and use what He has given you. No, it is not easy to jump into your calling, but you must be faithful and patient enough to allow God to train you and prepare you to do His kingdom work with power.

## Challenges, Obstacles, and Setbacks Make Us Strong in the Lord

On our way to operating in the gifts God has placed within us, we may suffer through some distressing experiences. But if we trust God and His Word, those unpleasant experiences can be used by Him to turn things around for us and lead us to discover His purpose and will for our life.

Romans 8:28 clearly states, "All things work together for good for those who love God, and who are called according to his purpose or plan." Whenever the enemy tries to bring you down, remember that if you are in God and with God, God will cause bad things to work out for good for you. There is no need to fear, be disappointed, give up, or become bitter when you are going through some challenges in your life or ministry. Trust God. Instead of getting *bitter* when you go through difficult situations in life, get *better* at using what God has given you. Use His gifts to bless others and proclaim the goodness of Yahweh to all humanity. Don't get frustrated when things are not going the way you would like them to, but stand your ground and trust the Lord Adonai to turn any situation around for your good. Where the enemy wants to bring a curse in your life, God wants to bring a blessing. When the enemy closes one door, God will open another one—in fact, even a better door. With God on your side, the enemy cannot destroy the seed of life that is in you or stop you from doing what God has anointed you to do in life. Don't let fear of man and failure stop you from functioning in the power of your gifts.

We will look at obstacles again later in this book, but for now let me briefly share an inspirational and true-life experience with you. After hearing the voice of the Lord clearly telling him to leave his home country and move to America to study the Word of God to prepare for his kingdom assignment, Mukisa, a good friend of mine, hesitated. Several things made leaving his home country difficult. First, he was actively involved in ministry in his local church, where he served as an assistant youth pastor and actively served in evangelism. Second, he and his wife had just had their first child. Furthermore, he was uncomfortable with the thought of going to a foreign land without his family or friends. But then the Lord spoke to him a second time, saying, "If you go, I will go with you, and I will be with you all the way through. I want you to go and study my Word in depth and allow my Spirit to consume and transform you and empower you to do my work." He obeyed God's instructions. By faith he left his home country and enrolled in a Bible college. His wife and child joined him a year later.

Mukisa carefully followed God's instructions and dedicated his life to studying, understanding, and letting God's Word consume and transform his life. He did not seek ministry or ministry positions in the local church he had joined and actively attended; rather, his desire was to seek more of God's presence in his life. Things were not easy for him and his young family, but the Lord was faithful to be with him throughout. He provided for Mukisa by connecting him with kingdom-minded people who supported him through both prayers and financial help. When he finally graduated from the Bible college after six and a half years, he began waiting on God to tell him what to do next. He did what many people would have done—he waited and did nothing, instead of immediately beginning to put into practice what he had learned at college. Because He was not swiftly responding to God's call on his life, God started taking him on a journey to awaken His vision and will in Mukisa. The first awakening was when the pastor of the local church he was attending told him, "I haven't heard God tell me to give you anything to do in my church or to bring you on board as one of my staff members." Mukisa confidently and respectfully replied to the pastor, "Me neither, Pastor. I haven't heard God tell me to ask you to give me a ministry or to join the church staff, but I know God has something for me to do."

Your first thought may be that the man of God rejected Mukisa, but you need to look at the way God works sometimes to drive his people to His original plan for their life. Soon after the pastor had spoken to Mukisa, God used another man of God in the city to take

Mukisa on another experience. This man was leading a church and appointed Mukisa as director of that church's training program. By the grace of God, Mukisa excelled at that ministry, and he also began teaching part-time at a Bible college. Many people were touched and empowered by the Word of God. Mukisa began to think his calling was to teach in a Bible college. He slowly started forgetting God's original call to win souls for God's kingdom. However, I've learned God doesn't waste anything. He was using Mukisa's church work and college teaching to equip him and prepare him for his original assignment of winning souls.

Now watch this! Mukisa became comfortable in his position as a training director and college teacher and gradually lost sight of God's original vision for his life. Then God used the first pastor, who had earlier told him he had not heard from God about Mukisa, to get him back on track. That man of God called him and told him God had given him a vision of Mukisa as a leader of evangelism at his church. Mukisa humbly accepted that role after being released by the other church and the Bible college. That year he was asked to lead the church missions team to Africa for some evangelistic work. He led the team, and God did wonders through them on that mission trip. Many people gave their lives to the Lord Jesus Christ, and many more were set free from the power and influence of Satan. But when Mukisa returned with the team after the successful trip, the pastor told him the church was not going to pursue world mission work anymore. Mukisa felt disappointed and even betrayed, but immediately the Holy Spirit said to him, "I sent you on that mission trip to show you what I have called you to do and what I am calling you to do." So instead of being upset, disappointed, bitter, or resentful about the pastor's decision, Mukisa suddenly saw what God was calling him to do, and his vision and passion were revived by the power of the Holy Spirit.

Once God had revived Mukisa's vision and renewed his call, Mukisa ran with God's vision. Immediately God started using him effectively to impact countless people's lives around the world through the power of the gospel. Just as God had promised, He opened many doors for Mukisa and brought kingdom-minded people into his life who supported him with prayer and finances as he preached the gospel. Opposition and slander from a few jealous religious individuals could not stop him from obeying God's call. God had captured his heart, and there was nothing the devil could do to stop the work of God being accomplished in and through Mukisa. Those difficult challenges he had faced earlier did not break him down but rather built him up into a stable and faithful servant of God. God had used the unpleasant moments Mukisa passed through to propel him to his destiny and calling in life. To this day, this servant of God is reaching multitudes of people for Christ all over the world because he is fulfilling the purpose for which God consecrated him. He is making an impact in the lives of many people because he is using his God-given gifts as God designed them—to bless God's people and not to elevate himself.

The enemy may try to stop you or even incite people against you, but don't allow bitterness or anger to pollute your heart. Rejection, slander, or opposition can never kill the gifts of God in you if you focus on the One who created you and called you according to His grace and power.

Jesus said this to His disciples,

> I am sending you out like sheep among wolves. Therefore be as **shrewd as serpents** and **as harmless as doves**. Because people will hand you over to sanhedrins and flog you in their synagogues, beware of them. You will even be brought before governors and kings because of Me, to bear witness to them

and to the nations. But when they hand you over, don't worry about how or what you should speak. For you will be given what to say at that hour, because you are not speaking, but the Spirit of your Father is speaking through you. Brother will betray brother to death, and a father his child. Children will even rise up against their parents and have them put to death. You will be hated by everyone be cause of my name. **But the one who endures to the end will be delivered.** (Matthew 10:16–22, boldface added)

This profound scripture is extremely important to every disciple of Jesus Christ. Jesus was shedding light on the reality of His disciples living in an ungodly world, while at the same time showing them how to withstand the tactics of the enemy and get to the finish line of proclaiming the good news. He disclosed to the disciples that He was sending them out like sheep among wolves. Just as wolves stalk, hunt, and try to kill the sheep, Satan through persecution would attempt to hunt and destroy them; thus, they must be careful and smart as serpents. Serpents are shrewd because they can detect danger and flee from it quickly. The disciples must be able to detect danger and flee from one city to another and continue to spread the good news of the kingdom (Matthew 10:23). As you embark on a journey to do the work of God, Satan will try everything possible to stop the will of God for your life using tactics such as rejection, persecution, opposition, and slander. Furthermore, he will try to destroy the seed of life God has placed within you, but you must be smart and quick to discern his schemes so you don't fall into his traps.

When we are going through challenging times, it is difficult to remain focused on Jesus Christ and His mission for us. Many people give up along the way, while others become frustrated, agitated, and upset when they face opposition. Thus, they respond by attacking back through ungodly words. But we must understand that our battle is not against flesh and blood but against the spiritual forces of evil in the heavenly realms (Ephesians 6:12). We are not to go after those who oppose us, because they are not our enemy; the real enemy camouflages himself and fights us through other people. We must fight him by putting on the full armor of God, which is the truth of the Word of God and the righteousness of Christ. We must fight him by proclaiming the gospel of peace to the nations. To preach the gospel of Jesus Christ with transforming power, we need to be as harmless as a dove to those who oppose us or treat us unfairly. Moreover, we also need to have unshakable faith. With the shield of faith in Jesus Christ and His power and ability to overcome the power of Satan, we can extinguish all the flaming arrows of the Evil One.

In every challenging situation, remain calm. Take the helmet of salvation and the sword of the Spirit, which is the Word of God, and pray always in the Spirit. This way you will persevere and focus on the task God has entrusted to you. As Christians, we live in a world full of wolves seeking to destroy the will of God for us and for the nations, but God in us and with us (Immanuel) will protect us. As you step out to do God's will, be assured that He will go with you and empower you if you put your trust in Him and in His Word. God is faithful. He will go ahead of you to prepare the way. And He will sustain you through the power of the Holy Spirit so you can bring honor and glory to His name.

When the Lord called the children of Israel out of Egypt, He was there to guide them during the day with a pillar of cloud and by night in a pillar of fire. Your God is with you. He will guide you during the day when your life is going well. He will guide you in the darkest moments of your life, lighting the path ahead of you and making a way for you. Sometimes you may feel as though God is not with you when you are facing challenges, but the truth is that God is always close to you in times of trouble. He even commands His angels to look after you. So don't give up, feel abandoned, or lose heart. Our great God is a present help in times of trouble. He is and will always be there with you.

Second Corinthians 4:1 says, "Through God's mercy we have a ministry of not losing heart." Satan's goal is to bring stumbling blocks into our life to derail us from standing on the truth of the gospel of Jesus Christ and from serving in the kingdom of God. But when we know the divine power of God operating in our lives through the Holy Spirit, we can never give up on propagating the good news of the kingdom. It is through the divine power of God (not our own strength) that we can stand firm and strong on the Word of God and in the presence of the almighty God when the going becomes difficult. Because of the divine power of the kingdom of God, we may be pressed on every side but not crushed, perplexed but not in despair, because nothing can defeat our God.

In my personal experience I have discovered that one of the keys to not losing heart when things get difficult is depending on the divine power of God available through the gentle and yet powerful Holy Spirit. We must understand that the kingdom of God is a kingdom full of supernatural power. Knowing this should give us strength and boldness to serve Him faithfully in any situation. Without the power of God working in our life, it is impossible for us to function powerfully in our God-given gifts or to do what God has called us to do for His kingdom. Furthermore, it is through the power of God and of His Spirit that we can step out in faith to help and serve others with our gifts. Sadly, many Christians today don't know how to let the power of the kingdom of God rule and reign in their lives and enable them to do the work of God.

Rejection from other people has no power to stop God's purpose for your life. Your God and creator has the final say in your life, so never say *never* if God hasn't said so. Keep marching forward and doing what God has called you to do with a humble heart and a servant's attitude. Challenges, setbacks, and obstacles are inevitable, but when you stand your ground and faithfully believe the Word of God, they can lead to victory and open doors.

## God Is Waiting for You to Function in the Power of His Spirit

Many people fear doing the work of God because of opposition and rejection by people. Well, if God has indeed called you to step out of the ordinary and function in His extraordinary power and ability, then you need fear no more. God will be with you to protect you, watch over you, and empower you to do His work. You are a missing piece of "wood" on the fireplace that God would like to set ablaze. He wants the local church to be on fire for Him and be His voice to the world. God is saying this to you right now as you read this book: "If you go, I will go with you. I will make a way for you, and I will provide for you." God is waiting on you. He is waiting to use you, but you must step out in faith to do what He has called you to do in the body of Christ. You are not called just to watch everyone else do the work of ministry. You are called to function in the body of Christ in whatever area God has graciously gifted you for.

Yes, you may need some training, some character building, and greater understanding of the true character and nature of God to effectively do the work of God and serve Him in both humility and power. But remember this: God stands ready to use you powerfully and to move in you and through you. He is waiting for you to step out willingly in faith and allow Him to capture your heart. If you just sit there and do nothing, waiting for someone to give you a ministry or just complaining about the spiritual condition of the world and the church, then you will be complaining for many years. Jesus is waiting for you to declare His Word in the spiritual realm and speak life to every spiritually dry and dead person to live again. God is ready to use you, but are you ready to step out in faith? Don't limit what God intends to do through your life; He is waiting on you to go into the world and do His work in the power of His Spirit. Not everyone is called into full-time ministry—this we know for sure—but God has anointed every individual Christian with gifts that are critical to the body of Christ. Whatever your gifts may be, use them to extend the kingdom of God.

In our next chapter we will examine how we can allow the dynamic power of God's reign to flow in us and through us so we can step into our divine calling and be fruitful in life. Through His power we can become fearless and be all He has called us to be for His kingdom. What can stop us? Fear of the unknown. Fear of man. A lack of knowledge about the power of God that is resident in us. Where there is no knowledge of the power of God, people live purposeless and weak lives. Without the power of the Holy Spirit, we can't serve God or live an overcoming, fruit-bearing life. Without God's power, there is no healing, no transformation, and basically no life. It is only through the power of God that we can have courage, determination, kingdom purpose, and focus. It is only through the power of God that we can have passion to be a channel through whom He can bring healing, transformation, deliverance, and change to the nations. When we discover the power of the Holy Spirit, we discover strength and stability to live for God and serve Him. As you continue to read this book, my prayer is that you will discover the power of God on your life and begin to live life from a position of victory instead of defeat. When the power and favor of God are with you, it doesn't matter what the enemy throws at you or what life throws at you—because God's power is supreme and conquers all things.

Life is full of storms. When your storm is big, your testimony will be even bigger because of the power of God reigning in you. The power of God in you will give you a beautiful song of victory to sing during and after the storm, because God is the one who fights for you and gives you victory. Instead of living in despair when you are going through a stormy season, you will live with hope, courage, and determination and withstand the storms without being shaken by them.

This is your season and time to rise above every setback and challenge and become all God destined you to be. Let the Holy Spirit rule and reign in you, and you will live a successful and fruitful life in the Lord. With God's power you can do and be all He has called you to do and be and can thrive in His presence.

## Chapter 2

# WHEN GOD REIGNS IN YOU

You Can't Remain Quiet Any Longer

In this chapter we will focus on how to allow the reign of God to rule in us and manifest its power through us so we can rise up in the power of the name of God and fearlessly do the work He has called each of us to do. This work involves proclaiming the goodness of God's kingdom to all people of all nations with signs and wonders. This must be done in humility and with a compassionate heart full of the love of God.

Many of us are afraid to step out and be all God has called us to be because we fear criticism or feel unqualified or don't believe we are called to do the work of God. Such thinking leads us to feel more comfortable and secure in just being church attendees waiting to go to heaven. But God has not called us just to *go* to church but to *be* the church—to actively win souls for Him.

God wants us to reign with Him here on earth. That is why He has appointed us to be a kingdom and priests (Revelation 5:10). What is stopping us from reigning with God? Fear. Fear is a theme we will return to frequently in this book simply because it is a major and common hindrance to living in the power of God. Where fear reigns, people are afraid to do anything, but where the Spirit of God reigns, people are bold and ready to confront any giants. If you fear God, honor His name, and love what He loves (people), you have nothing to fear.

**Bold and Courageous—No Fear of Giants**

In 1 Samuel 17:1–25 we read the amazing story of the small, young, and unskilled David defeating the great, skilled, and giant Philistine warrior Goliath. But how was that possible? From a human viewpoint, David had no chance of defeating Goliath. If we are to learn a valuable and important lesson in this account, however, we need to discover the *power* and *motivation* behind David's courage and success against the giant. David was still a young man and unskilled in warfare. However, he had the audacity to challenge the mighty Goliath to battle, even though the entire well-trained and well-prepared army of Israel had watched helplessly in fear for forty days at the battlefront as Goliath challenged and taunted the Israelites. The army of Israel struggled not only to find a man to challenge Goliath but also to find the motivation and courage to go after him. That brings us to this question: Where did David find the courage, motivation, and determination to step up and step out to challenge Goliath? Was David just a prideful and arrogant young man who didn't know the threat Goliath posed? No. The drive behind David's motivation and courage was not found in self or personal strength but in God and in the power of His name—a power that had rescued David from lions and bears. When you know God and you know His power and believe in His powerful name without doubting anything, your motivation level and courage increase beyond human strength and understanding.

When Eliab, David's older brother, overheard his younger brother inquiring about the prize that would be given to the man who killed the giant Philistine, he was angry. He asked David, "Why did you come down here? Who is watching those few sheep in the wilderness? I know your arrogance and your evil heart—you came down to see the battle" (1 Samuel 17:28). Eliab misjudged David's intentions. He considered him arrogant because David lacked the military training or qualifications he and the other soldiers had and yet wanted to take on the giant warrior Goliath. When King Saul learned David wanted to go out and fight the Philistine, he said to the boy, "You can't go fight this Philistine. You're just a youth, and he's been a warrior since he was young" (1 Samuel 17:33). David was not an arrogant, prideful, or egotistical person, and his confidence was not in himself. David simply knew Someone who could empower him to tame and silence Goliath, and His name was Yahweh, the God of Israel. Boldness and courage come from knowing Yahweh—the God of all power.

David declared no enemy had the right to taunt or mock the name of the living and Holy God or His people and go unpunished. Because of Yahweh's influence in David's life, he refused to just sit and watch quietly as Goliath taunted his God and his people. He had to act out of God's power and strength, not out of a military training or background, which he lacked. Furthermore, David went after Goliath because he feared God more than he feared the giant. Again, when we fear God and love what He loves and hate what He hates, there is nothing more to fear, and nothing can hold us captive in life. Jesus tells us in Matthew 10:28, "Do not fear those who kill the body but are unable to kill the soul: but rather fear Him [God] who is able to destroy both soul and body in hell." Criticism or hatred should never stop you from pursuing God or from allowing Him to work through you to bring deliverance to those around you. Be bold and courageous.

## When God's Power Reigns in You, All Things Are Possible

Here is an important observation: a person can have training, educational degrees, and skills and yet struggle and fail to succeed in life. A person's training or qualifications do not guarantee victory because in the kingdom of God victory is achieved only through the power of God. This does not mean we don't need to be trained or educated. God can work through the things we learn that way. The problem comes when we rely solely on what we have learned and think we can succeed without God. No matter how much training we have, without the presence and power of God reigning in our life, we are powerless to overcome life's obstacles or gain victory against spiritual Goliaths in our life. Victory over the enemy—both spiritual and physical—can be achieved by allowing the God of all power to reign and rule in our life. That is why David told King Saul how the Lord's power had rescued David from the lion and the bear when he was tending his father's sheep. In the strength and mighty power of God, David had rescued lambs from these animals and killed them both (1 Samuel 17:34–37).

David believed these experiences made him the right person to handle a bigger problem such as Goliath, who had defied the Israelite army for forty days. David made his case clearly to the king, that the same God who had rescued him before would not only rescue him now against Goliath but also give him victory over the giant.

David's courage and determination puzzled everyone around him then and puzzle many people to this day. But those people don't understand David's source of courage, determination, and faith that he could defeat Goliath. David's courage and determination emerged from the powerful name of God and God's ability to do above and beyond what man's strength or ability can do. Therefore, the focal point in this account is on God and His unmatched power and strength. Goliath was like a mountain that the Israelites could not level or climb, but the young David defeated him because his eyes were on God's power, not Goliath's. David's faith, courage, and determination were in the name and power of God.

By enabling David to defeat Goliath without any military skills, training, or weapons, Yahweh, the God of Israel, demonstrated that all battles, spiritual or physical, must be fought in the power of His name, which is superior to any other name or power in heaven or on earth. It is important to understand the three things that played a major role in the life of David and led him to step up and challenge Goliath:

- The reign of God in him, which would not allow him to ignore Goliath
- The power of God David had witnessed and experienced as a shepherd
- David's reverence for and faith in the holy name of God

The account of David and Goliath teaches us many things, but above all it teaches us that God's power is superior to all other powers. When His power reigns in our life, we cannot stand back in fear but rather must rise in the power of God and be a channel through whom God's power can be demonstrated. In life, all we need is to trust God and to live in the power and strength of His name because with God all things are possible. Nothing is too difficult for Him.

When God reigns in our life, the impossible suddenly becomes possible. Throughout history God has a track record of doing supernatural and impossible things. The following scriptures should inspire you to stand in the power of the name of God.

> "Is anything too difficult for the Lord?" (Genesis 18:14 NASB)

"Ah Lord God! Behold, you have made the heavens and the earth by your great power and by your outstretched arm! Nothing is too difficult for you." (Jeremiah 32:17 NASB)

"For nothing will be impossible with God." (Luke 1:37)

Describing what God is capable of doing, Job said, "I know that you can do all things, and that no purpose of yours can be thwarted" (Job 42:2 NASB). Job had previously questioned God's actions (see Job 16:12–14), but he came back to his senses and declared that God was powerful over all matters, including his situation. God's power can still turn around your situation and fight your battles. He never changes; He is the same yesterday, today, and forevermore. No one can defeat God. And no one can defeat you if God is on your side. That's why it is so important to let God alone rule and reign in your life.

Without God we are destined for defeat at the hands of the enemy. Being religious or attending a church service does not guarantee victory. Victory comes only by allowing the King of kings and the Lord of lords, Jesus Christ, to live in and through you and influence your life. This doesn't mean you will be perfect, but where the presence and anointing of Jesus Christ are, there is perfection—because our perfection is in Him and not in our self-righteousness. Let Him rule, and let Him have His own way in you. Only then will you live a victorious life of serving God.

## Don't Be Silent—Let the Holy Spirit Reign in You!

Another valuable lesson we learn from the account of David and Goliath is that family members, friends, religious leaders, and people in general may misunderstand your confidence, zeal, and passion for the Lord. They may judge you to be arrogant, prideful, and even rebellious because you are not doing things their way. But never forget that man's ways are not God's ways and man's thoughts are not God's thoughts (Isaiah 55:8). Just because man rejects you or your ways doesn't mean God does. Man looks at the outward appearances, while God looks at the heart's intentions (1 Samuel 16:7). If you do things to bring honor, fame, and glory to the name of God, you have nothing to worry about. But if you do things to look good, to please people, or to achieve fame or glory, then by all means pay attention when criticism comes because it can save both your life and the lives of those around you.

Jesus was criticized and called names. The religious leaders heavily criticized His disciples and eventually caused death for many of them, but this did not stop them from proclaiming the arrival of the kingdom of God. Most of the people who criticized Jesus' followers were "religious." They thought they knew God and His ways better than anyone else, but God is God. He cannot be confined to a box or limited to a certain way of doing things. He is God, and He can use anybody to do His will—regardless of the person's religious or cultural background—*if* the person has a heart for the things of God.

Therefore, do not be silenced by the critics or intimidated by your lack of education or your cultural background. Just allow the Holy Spirit of God to reign in you and spark a kingdom fire in your heart. When the Holy Spirit reigns in your heart and flows through your life, it is impossible for you to remain unfruitful, dormant, or silent. You cannot keep from testifying of the goodness of God or proclaiming the power of the gospel of Jesus Christ that has transformed and consumed you. The blaze of the Holy Spirit comes to ignite your passion for Jesus Christ and His kingdom so it cannot be contained. This fire, or passion, becomes our fuel, or motivation, to do the work of God.

We don't do the work of the kingdom of God because we are perfect or more gifted or righteous or spiritually educated than others. We rise to do the work of God because of His grace, Jesus' righteousness, and the power of the Holy Spirit. The greatest way to show our appreciation for what God has done in our life is to respond to His graciousness by testifying of His goodness to others. If God has transformed you and you are grateful for what He has done, then it is impossible for you to be silenced by opposition. The apostles Peter and John said it well: "But Peter and John answered them, 'Whether it's right in the sight of God for us to listen to you rather than to God, you decide; for we are unable to stop speaking about what we have seen and heard'" (Acts 4:19-20).

Before the disciples of Jesus Christ could go out to proclaim the gospel (good news) that their master, Jesus Christ, had proclaimed, He had to prepare them to encounter opposition, hatred, rejection, and even death. He did so by providing them with the power of the Holy Spirit. In Matthew 10:22 Jesus stated, "You will be hated by everyone on account of my name, but the one who perseveres to the end will be saved." And in Matthew 24:9 He stated, "Then will they hand you over to be persecuted and killed, and you will be hated by all nations on account of my name." Ironically, this persecution would come not from nonreligious people but from religious circles. The disciples needed the power of the Holy Spirit to come upon them and burn within them so they could go out and make an impact for the kingdom of God in Jerusalem, Judea, Samaria, and the remotest parts of the earth (Acts 1:8)—*even amid the storm of opposition*. You may experience opposition and resistance as you follow Jesus Christ, but with the power of the Holy Spirit working in you and for you, you will not be silenced or stopped from doing what the Word of God commands you to do.

*Dr. Kazumba Charles*

## Trained to Serve in the Kingdom of God

Many Christians find it challenging to function in their spiritual gifts or use them serving in a local church. Consequently, they move from one church to another in search of a one where they can learn to serve in the kingdom of God in a practical way. But I have personally observed that people can change churches or cities or countries and still fail to function in their spiritual gifts. I have also discovered that people who attend a church where they are trained to serve in the kingdom of God can change their place of worship or geographic location and still continue to serve. The key can often be found in training—or a lack of training.

Training is essential for people to serve efficiently in the kingdom of God. We must be trained—not "preached to" but trained— to serve. We must be equipped with the Word of God. We must be encouraged and supported to use what we have learned. Then it becomes easier to serve in the kingdom of God and to make an impact in the world. But if we are not trained or equipped to serve, we will struggle to serve and will continue to struggle in our spiritual lives and usually settle for being church spectators and not participators.

In the Christian world today we see many Christians who have been preached to about serving but not properly trained. Preaching about serving and training them to do it are two very different things. Preaching about serving does not necessarily give a person an opportunity to serve—it only calls or inspires a person to service. Training must follow. A trained person is encouraged and helped to put the training into practice. Lack of training prevents many believers in Christ from knowing how to use their gifts for the benefit of the body of Christ, and consequently they do not know how to function in the kingdom of God or be of service to their local church.

Many people are willing to serve, but they are not trained or equipped to do so. Instead, they are trained to sit down and be good listeners of the Word, which is great but not enough to make the body of God effective. In fact, this tends to produce nothing but spiritually knowledgeable people who comfortably sit in their church pews Sunday after Sunday but make little impact on society. Jesus trained His disciples to serve, not to sit down and do nothing or just cheer for Him. As disciples of Jesus Christ, our desire and goal should be to study and learn the Word of God—not only for the knowledge but also so we can do God's work. Teachers of the Word of God should be passionate about equipping people to be what God created them to be and not what we want them to be.

Serving God corporately begins by equipping and training believers in Christ in the Word with a focus on equipping them to become a functional part of the body of Christ. This requires the trainer to support and encourage his or her students to go out there and do the work of God while getting them involved in the activities of the local church using their gifts. Proverbs 22:6 says, "Teach a youth about the way he should go; even when he is old he will not depart from it." This scripture is not about training the youth to behave but rather training them in the true wisdom of God (Proverbs 4:11) so when they are fully grown they will never depart from functioning in the ways and wisdom of God. As already stated, teachers or preachers of the Word of God should focus on teaching the Word to people, with a view to equipping them to be functioning parts of the body of Christ, not only in their local church but also outside the local church. Furthermore, each disciple of Jesus Christ is responsible for developing a willing heart and teachable attitude so we can all reign and rule with Yahweh here on earth in the splendor of His majestic power and anointing.

*Dr. Kazumba Charles*

## Jesus Came to Make Fire-Filled Disciples—Not Pew-Warmers

Jesus did not come to make pew-warmers. He trained and raised up disciples who believed in Him and would follow in His footsteps and do even greater works. In John 14:12 He said to His disciples, "I assure you: The one who believes in me will do the works that I do. And he will do even greater works than these, because I am going to the Father." If we believe in Jesus, then we ought to do *something* for the kingdom of God. And, indeed, because of Jesus' finished work on the cross, His disciples—then and now—can do even greater works. Greater works cannot be done by pew-warmers. Greater works are done only by believers who are not afraid to step out and let Jesus shine through them.

James 1:22 challenges every believer in Christ to be not a mere listener of the Word of God but a doer. Change in the world requires someone doing something to bring it about. Change happens when the people of God rise up in the anointing of God. If you want to make a difference in the world and in your family, as well as in your own life, then you must move beyond being just a listener and become a doer of the Word.

Furthermore, you need to allow the Holy Spirit to inscribe God's Word on your heart so you can become what God is calling every Christian to be: a dynamic person of God full of kingdom life, peace, and hope. In Deuteronomy 11:18–19 God commanded His people to imprint His words on their hearts and on their souls and to bind them as a sign on their hands and as a symbol on their foreheads. Moreover, they were to teach the Lord's words to their children by talking about them when they sat in their houses, when they walked along the road, when they lay down, and when they got up. Why? Because when the Word of God is inscribed on our heart, mind, soul, and body, we find it easier to talk about the goodness of God, to obey His Word, to teach His Word, and to live out His instruction. When we obey the Word of God, we have room in our life to reign, to rule, and to do the His work in His power.

The presence of God's Word and its power should change us from idle listeners into active servants of God. When we study Jesus' teachings about the kingdom of God, we find that His goal as He trained His disciples was to spark a passionate fire in them for doing the works of the kingdom of God within their communities and beyond. After the disciples heard their Master's words, they were ignited with a passion for God. When we hear and do the Word, our faith springs into action, opening ourselves to the supernatural influence and empowerment of the Holy Spirit to do extraordinary works of God. Imagine for a second a situation where all believers in Christ are trained and motivated to do the work of God and allowed to use their gifts to build and advance God's kingdom. No doubt the world would be lit up with the presence of God and we would see healing, deliverance, and transformation as never before in our lives and in the world.

**Why Do We Need the Reign of God?**

We all face life challenges and spiritual battles. We cannot go far or win a battle without the presence and reign of God's power in our life. As a disciple of Jesus Christ, your life is like that of an athlete. No athlete trains or practices day in and day out only to sit on the bench. And no true athlete lacks the desire to compete in the championship game. Every athlete trains to play and win at all cost. For that reason, a serious athlete spends hours in training. A trainer or coach does not assemble a team and train them without a plan that focuses on winning games. A sports club hires a coach to train, equip, and prepare the team for each game. And for the team to be competitive and win games, the coach must develop every talent available to him and place the players in the positions they best fit.

This is the same pattern Jesus employed. He assembled His disciples and began to coach (train) them. He revealed to them the mysteries of the kingdom of God so they could defeat the kingdom of darkness. Jesus invested much time in training and equipping His disciples so that after He had gone to His Father in heaven, those disciples (Team Jesus) would continue to implement the government of God here on earth. The power that raised Jesus Christ from the dead would live and reign in them (Romans 8:11).

As a disciple of Jesus Christ, you are like an athlete. You must dedicate yourself to train your mind, soul, and body with the Word of God so you can participate in the kingdom of God as a team player. The key to being a successful team player in the kingdom of God is knowing your position in Christ and operating in *your* gifting and not in someone else's. Know what your gifts are and spend time developing them so you can effectively serve in the kingdom of God. It is dangerous not knowing or operating in your area of gifting. In fact, it brings confusion, dissatisfaction, and disunity in the body of Christ. Know your gifts, and don't be jealous of someone else or try to compete with others.

In the kingdom of God there can be no competition, individualism, insecurities, jealousy, or superstars. The kingdom of God consists of disciples of Jesus Christ who are called to serve both God and His people in unity and as one body. Each church and believer has a position and a role to play for God and according to God's grace. No one is more or less important than another, even though the tasks and roles will vary. If we truly understand this, we can powerfully advance the kingdom of God and value one another as we should. God wants the body of Christ today to grasp this revelation: Churches, ministries, and Christians are not to compete with one another but are to rise up and reign with God in unity as the true body of Christ. Our spiritual race or battle is not against one another but against the spiritual forces of evil (Ephesians 6:12). Let us never forget that. Because we are fighting a spiritual battle, we need to stand in the power of God and function according to our gifts without any hindrance from within the body. With the reign of God at work, even the seemingly most dysfunctional parts of the body of Christ will be turned into functional parts of Christ's church.

## Turning the Dysfunctional into Functional Parts of the Body of Christ

As I minister around the world, I often hear church leaders say, "People don't like to serve in the church." The question is *Why?* History reveals the body of Christ constantly facing this issue. Many of these nonparticipants are faithful Christians who attend church services regularly but never move beyond that to become actively involved in the ministry of the church and the mission of God. Is it because they are prideful? Or do they lack resources, training, passion, or encouragement and trust from their leadership? Could they be weak in the Lord? Every church leader should try to discover why some people in the church are dysfunctional parts of the body or have a hard time committing their time, energy, or gifts to the body of Christ. Failure to discover the reasons can lead to assumptions, animosity, hostility, and a toxic environment between the leadership and the people they are entrusted to lead.

Many leaders assume that uninvolved attendees are simply rebellious, full of pride, and disobedient to church authority. This may be true in some cases, but not all nonparticipants can be characterized this way. In fact, many people *want* to serve in some capacity, but they don't know how they can do so. Most people just need guidance, trust, training, support, and coaching. Above all, they need an encounter with the presence and power of God to awaken their gifts and passion for the things of God. The truth is that we cannot force people to serve if they do not have the spirit of service in them or enthusiasm or excitement for the kingdom of God.

Before rushing to condemn, judge, disqualify, or label people, leaders must find the reasons behind their unwillingness to serve and use their spiritual gifts. People serve in the kingdom of God and use their gifts when they are empowered to do so. Gifts or talents do not just develop on their own without being cultivated, nourished, and watered—and then polished and released to serve.

Some believers are afraid to get involved in the work of God because of past hurts they have experienced. The church is full of people who have experienced spiritual abuse or come from a background of hurt or life trauma. To expect such people to thrive and serve without proper training, leadership, encouragement, and spiritual healing is like trying to start a vehicle that has a dead battery. The engine is there, but the battery is dead. It takes a sensitive and visionary leader to understand that and to replace the dead battery (passion) with the spark of the Word of God by using the "jumper cables" of the Holy Spirit to ignite a kingdom drive in people's hearts. When we see people from God's perspective, we will find it easier to help, inspire, and motivate them, cultivating their gifts so they can serve God as He designed them to do.

We Christians sometimes forget that when one person struggles to serve God, the whole body of Christ is affected. The strength of the body is in the strength of each part that makes up the body. Consequently, when an individual struggles, it is no surprise that the corporate body struggles too. When we realize this, our self-centered attitudes that degrade and criticize other believers or churches that may be struggling in their service to God suddenly disappear. We may come from different denominations, but the struggles of other believers and other churches are our struggles and affect us too, since we are all part of one body—the body of Christ. Jesus did not bring denominations into the world. He brought the kingdom of God, and we are all part of that kingdom. Therefore, we must not compete with one another or laugh at other believers who fall in their walk with Jesus Christ. Rather we should encourage and help one another. We should lift one another up when we fall short so together we can serve the kingdom of God. Philippians 2:3 commands us to act not out of selfish ambition or pride but in humility and to count others as better than ourselves. This kind of attitude ignites a fire, a passion, and instills confidence both in others and in us to serve God in unity and love. This is what turns the dysfunctional into functional parts of the body of Christ.

## Why Do People Struggle to Serve?

Several issues keep people from using their God-given gifts and serving in the kingdom of God. These things also prevent people from rising up in the power of God.

### *A Negative Environment*

Places of worship where the spirit of slander, manipulation, control, gossip, name-calling, hatred, jealousy, and strife are preeminent automatically switch people off from serving God in truth and in Spirit and cause them to struggle to live for God. But where there is a spirit of love, kindness, gentleness, self-control, and honor both for God and for one another, people's passion to serve is ignited and their gifts produce fruits. Such an environment produces the confidence and courage required to turn the dysfunctional into functional parts of the body. When rebuke or correction is done with gentleness, in love and honor for God and for one another, people become loyal servants of God and are grateful for godly spiritual leadership.

As an individual, if you want to serve God powerfully, find a place where the Spirit of God is evident so you can grow and cultivate your gifts to serve in the kingdom of God. As a leader, desire to create a place of worship where the Spirit of God can rule and reign both in your life and in the lives of those God has entrusted to you to lead to the streams of living water.

*The Attitude That They Are Useless*

It is amazing to see how many people feel, or have been made to feel, that they have nothing to offer to the kingdom of God—that their gifts are useless. But no God-given gifts are useless. Just because you are not a preacher, prophet, or apostle does not mean you are not gifted or you are useless. Think again of David. He was not in the army of Israel, and he was not trained as the soldiers of Israel would have been at the time of his battle with Goliath. His brother even tried to make him feel useless, saying, "Why did you come down here? Who did you leave those few sheep with in the wilderness? I know your arrogance and your evil heart—you came down to see the battle" (1 Samuel 17:28). David had a choice. He could feel useless and be quiet because of his lack of qualifications, or he could allow his passion and zeal for the name of God to make a difference.

The spirit of uselessness discourages people from serving God or using their gifts. In most cases people feel useless because of negative things that have been spoken about them or to them. They have been told they are nothing, they are not gifted as some other person, they are not good enough, or their past disqualifies them. The effect of this is compounded when there is a lack of proper training in

Scripture and in understanding that all believers in Christ have been given gifts to serve God.

God, of course, has selected specific people to lead and train believers in the Word of God and the ways of God so they can serve God and God alone. These Christian leaders are there to lead God's people to serve God and be a channel through whom the will of God in heaven is manifested here on earth. However, serving God is not just for a select few, such as pastors, evangelists, apostles, and teachers. Serving God is for all who have been redeemed from the kingdom of darkness into the kingdom of light and have received the power of the Holy Spirit.

Individuals who feel useful and recognize the measure of grace on their life are not afraid to step out and do what God has called them to do. However, when those who feel useless or not gifted enough to serve join a local church, they struggle to fit in and use their gifts. Often they are satisfied to be attendees and not participants. Christians must be careful not to rush to conclusions about individuals who don't serve in the kingdom of God. Many of these people are convinced they are not qualified to serve in a ministry capacity or to do anything for God. The last thing they need is a judgmental spirit aimed toward them. They need a Spirit-filled person who has the heart and love of God to come alongside them and encourage them through prayer support and exhortation in the Word of God.

When Jesus called His first disciples, He did not call men who were already qualified. We are told in Matthew 4:18–22 that He called mere fishermen: "Come follow me, and I will make you fishers of men." Undoubtedly, these fishermen felt useless as fishers of men, but the Teacher, Jesus Christ, was going to take that useless feeling away from them by equipping them with the power of the Word of God and revealing the mysteries of the kingdom of God to them.

God still specializes in qualifying the unqualified and calling the uncalled. Remember: He does not look at the outward appearance but at the willingness of the heart to serve Him. If you have been disqualified by people or feel as if you are useless, you need to learn what Peter taught. In 1 Peter 4:10 he wrote that God has given each of us a gift and that as good managers of the grace of God, we should use that gift to serve others. As a believer in Christ, you are not useless. You may not be a preacher, an apostle, a prophet, a teacher, or an evangelist, but you have a divine endowment that God has graciously entrusted to you as a good steward. You are responsible to use it to the glory of God without fear. All you need is a willing heart, a trainable spirit, and a humble attitude.

*They Are Hurting Spiritually or Emotionally*

No doubt many people in the church have been hurt and are still hurting spiritually and emotionally. When a person's spirit has been crushed, serving God becomes a challenge. Proverbs 18:14 puts it this way: "A man's spirit can endure sickness, but who can survive a broken spirit?" A broken or suffering spirit cannot willingly serve or function in the body of Christ. When you have a broken leg, you can't run or walk on it normally until it is properly healed. The same is true in the spiritual world. When you are spiritually hurting, you can't flow in the things of God. You first need to be healed by the Spirit of God. People may be struggling to use their gifts because of hurts and wounds they are carrying. Proverbs 17:22 says, "A joyful heart is good medicine, but a broken spirit dries up the bones." Dried-up bones here refers to people who have lost their vitality. When people lose their vitality for the things of God, they become stationary and are unwilling to do anything for God.

Spiritual wounds cause many people to hesitate to get involved in the activities of the local church or participate in the work of God.

Healing and help—not condemnation—should be our goal for these members of the body of Christ. Condemnation does not solve any problem, but encouragement and love do. They bring the motivation and healing required to serve God with a clean and pure heart. Church leadership should be gracious and provide the help needed to bring spiritually hurting people into a place of healing. The time to serve will come, but they need to be served first.

Often those who are hurting feel as if they are alone, abandoned, and powerless to do anything for the kingdom of God. Allow the Holy Spirit to show you ways you can help bring healing and restoration to them. Spiritually broken people need love, encouragement, and healing if they are to become involved in any work of God again—they don't need harsh words. Hebrews 10:24 says, "Let us be concerned about one another in order to promote love and good work." When believers care for one another, people will not forsake the gathering of the church (Hebrews 10:25). People want to be where love and encouragement are demonstrated. Nobody wants to serve in a place where he or she is constantly put down or discouraged.

People have reasons for not being actively involved in the ministry of the local body. The reasons are not the same for each person. Therefore, it is up to the leadership of the church to determine who in the congregation is struggling to serve because they feel useless and need encouragement … or because they are hurting and need healing and deliverance … or for some other reason. When compassionate leaders discern the problems and address individual needs, the fire to follow and serve God can again burn in the hearts of these people.

The church has been commissioned by Jesus to make disciples, not religious folks. The only way we can accomplish that task beyond the walls of our church is by having engaged, involved, and active disciples within the walls first. If you are a believer who has been hurt and spiritually broken by people, seek healing and deliverance so you can recover your passion for Jesus Christ. Don't allow people to kill the gifts of God or His calling on your life. Cry out to God, and He will pour out His healing rain on your life and mend your brokenness so you can do His work and live for Him alone. Whatever your hurts may be, my prayer is for healing and deliverance in your life by the power of God so you are set on fire for Him once again.

**What Is God's Reign?**

God's purpose for believers in Christ is not that they be religious, or just nice Christians, or churchgoers with some knowledge of Him who are eagerly waiting to be raptured away from earth. While God is concerned about people going to heaven, He is also concerned about getting heaven into people's hearts so His will can manifest itself in them as it is in heaven. When people discern the will of God, they cannot be silenced because God burns within them and they are fearless. Thus, God's priority for humankind is for His kingdom to rule and reign in their lives. That brings us to this question: What does *God's reign* mean? This is a significant question because only when we understand what the reign of God is can we let God's kingdom reign and rule in us.

The word *reign* refers to the influence, rule, or authority of a king or people. *God's reign* refers to His influence and authority over people or things. The Hebrew word is *malkut,* which may be rendered *reign,* or *kinghood,* or *kingdom.* So when we speak of God's reign in us, we are talking about God's influential power and authority taking charge of our spirit, mind, soul, and body. When God's power takes over our life, we become supercharged in our spirit and empowered to do things on behalf of God that we couldn't do within our own strength. A good example can be drawn from Acts 10:38, where

Peter spoke of "how God anointed Jesus of Nazareth with the Holy Spirit and power, and how he went about doing good healing all who were oppressed by the devil, because God was with him" (ISV). When God anointed Jesus Christ with the Holy Spirit, His power to reign took charge of Jesus so He could go and do good by healing everyone under the influence of the kingdom of darkness.

It must be emphasized that the kingdom of God is not a physical place but rather the rule and reign of God in the hearts of people. When God reigns in you, His influence, Spirit, and nature take over your life and empower you to do His work with extraordinary energy. When He reigns in you, you can't keep quiet because His impact on your life is too much to contain in your heart. Jeremiah had such an encounter with the reign of God. Here is what he said: "If I say, 'I won't mention Him or speak any longer in His name,' His message becomes a fire burning in my heart, shut up in my bones. I become tired of holding it in, and I cannot prevail" (Jeremiah 20:9). Each time Jeremiah felt like giving up and no longer speaking on behalf of God, the power of God's message that reigned in him became like a fire burning in his heart, shut up in his bones. Thus, he was influenced by the power of God to continue to speak the word of God.

What has silenced you in life? Is it people's mistreatment of you, or their gossip, or your own fear? God's power is more than powerful enough to dismantle all such hindrances and break you free to serve Him and help others find freedom too.

Jesus did great and mighty things in His short earthly ministry because of the power of God reigning in Him. The people He ministered to were living in darkness, but they saw a great light; a light dawned upon those who were living in the land of the shadow of death. Jesus' message was "Repent, for the kingdom of heaven is near" (Matthew 4:16–17). If we allow God to take control of our life and empower us, we can do great works of God by healing the sick and setting free those living in bondage to the power of darkness. If we are not seeing the manifest power of God flowing out of us, we have not yet allowed Him to flow in us and capture our heart. Remember—we can give only what we have. If the presence of God is in us, it will manifest itself through the words we speak, our love for people, and our passion for Jesus Christ and His kingdom. Here are just a few of the other benefits of Christ's reign in us:

- Pride—thinking of ourselves more highly than of others—disappears.
- Selfishness and selfish ambitions die.
- We live our life through God's power.
- We walk according to God's ways.
- Jealousy, competition, and hatred for one another disappear.
- We demonstrate the love and grace of God.
- The passion for Jesus Christ, His kingdom, and His words is rekindled.
- Our life is filled with God's purpose, will, and plan.

Allow the Holy Spirit of God to reign in you and break the dysfunctional spirit in your life, end the fruitlessness, and turn you into a fully functional and anointed part of the body of Christ. Let the Holy Spirit take full control of your life and let Him flow in and through you and revive your passion. And let the Word of God consume you, because when it consumes your heart, mind, soul, and body, nothing can stop you from glorifying Yahweh, your creator.

Your time to sit idle is over. It is time to arise in Jesus' name and reflect the glory of God and represent the kingdom of God. God alone empowers you, qualifies you, and heals you spiritually and emotionally. The beauty of the God we serve is that when He reigns over a person, sickness goes away, curses are turned into blessings, the weak are made strong, the unclean are cleansed, the unrighteous are made righteous, and the unqualified are qualified to declare the power of the kingdom of God. God's desire is to reign in you and me so that through us He can demonstrate His kindness to people. For too long we have lived our Christian lives without the power of God. It's time to discover or rediscover the power of God on our lives.

In the next chapter we will look at discovering your kingdom power. When you discover God's power in your life as a believer, no person or spiritual force of darkness can stop you from living for Him and using your gifts.

# Chapter 3

# DISCOVERING THE POWER OF GOD IN YOU

Overcoming Adversity and Thriving in Your Gifts

**The Power of God in You!**

One of the most gracious gifts God ever gave to humankind is the gift of salvation, which brings with it the power to live in His presence and the strength to do His will. While we can comprehend our salvation, given to us through the grace of God, many of us are yet to discover the power of God that comes with the package of salvation. God has not just saved us from the power of sin and death but has also given us His power to live out our salvation and thrive in Him. His power is crucial because it empowers us to be what He wants us to be and to do what He has called us to do here on earth. Our gifts, talents, knowledge, wisdom, vision, ideals, efforts, and plans are nothing without the backing of the power of God. The power of God is what makes things happen in the life of a Christian. When we discover the power of God in us, we recover everything the enemy has stolen from us and break through all the obstacles in life that stop us from excelling with God.

Most believers in Christ have come to know the power of God by reading about countless miracles and wonders in the Bible, yet many do not seem to understand that the same divine power that accomplished wonders back then is still available today. We can do even greater things because Christ lives in us. It is impossible to live for God or to please Him without His power. Consequently, God has not only saved us from the power of sin and death but has also infused us with His power and His Spirit and given us His Word so we can live in His Spirit and not in our flesh (see Romans 8:8–11). The presence of the Holy Spirit in us is the mark of God's power upon us. That power provides spiritual sustenance, gives life, strengthens us, guides us, and produces spiritual fruit in us. This means that when we discover our power in God and yield to its influence, we become dynamic, fearless, confident, bold, courageous, and full of the life of God. We have the power to withstand any conditions and to rescue others from the kingdom of darkness.

Trying to live a Christian life without the power of God leads to spiritual death or to being religious without any kingdom substance. Romans 8:13–14 says, "If you live according to the flesh, you will die; but if by the Spirit you put to death the deeds of the body, you will live. For all who are led by the Spirit of God are sons of God." We put the deeds of the flesh to death by the power of God through the work of the Holy Spirit. The deeds of the flesh (sins) that stop us from rising or moving forward in the Lord cannot be destroyed by our own strength or by our religion; they are defeated by allowing the power of God to work in us. The good news is that God has made His power available to us and we can fully walk in it. The power of God in our life also makes us tenderhearted, forgiving, gracious, compassionate, loving, humble, and caring. Let me again emphasize that living life or trying to do the work of God without the power of God is exhausting and dangerous.

By ourselves we have no strength or power to stand spiritually, advance the kingdom of God, or love God's people. It is the Holy Spirit alone who gives us such powers. With the power of God on our life, we can achieve things our earthly skills or training does not enable us to do. It is amazing and sad to see countless believers in Christ seek revival or try to make a difference in the world without the power of the Spirit of God. We need to turn back to God, seek Him, and surrender to His plans if we are to see revival and transformation in the world. Once we turn back to God and He turns back to us, the dynamic power He has placed within us will be revived.

One of the main reasons we live fearful, intimidated, and frustrated lives with no vision, no plan, and no purpose is that we don't understand the power of God within us. Realizing the magnitude of the power of God in us leaves no room for intimidating fear. Fear affects the functioning of our spiritual gifts and prevents us from producing kingdom fruit. Furthermore, fear of failure or being mocked can cause us to live our life in apathy, lukewarmness, and half-heartedness—uninvolved and uninterested in the things of God.

Don't be afraid of failing. People who have never failed have never tried anything new or stepped out of their comfort zone. The more you fear failure, the more you will fail! As long as we are here on earth, we will fail. But we who have been made righteous through Jesus Christ can fall seven times and still rise again (Proverbs 24:16) because God's power is so great He will not let us fail forever. As long as fear of failure abides in you, you will be spiritually stagnant, have little impact in society, and fail to live out your dreams or contribute positively to the body of Christ.

The church is full of world changers and kingdom shakers, but sadly most of them are timid and confined within the four walls of the church, while the outside world continues to suffer and perish spiritually. It is time to rediscover the power of God and its purpose in our life so we can break out of our comfort zone and demonstrate the characteristics of the kingdom of God in our communities. God's power, His presence in us, is not given to make us look more special than those who have not yet accepted God's salvation. It is not given so we can feel the goose bumps of the anointing of God. It is given to empower us to live as God's redeemed children and to enable us to do His will. God's power is for us, His disciples, to illustrate the gracious rule and reign of His kingdom and to declare to perishing souls the life of God and the hope that is in Christ when we receive Him as our Lord and Savior. Remembering this, we can boldly step out and reach out to people with God's grace.

**You Belong to a Powerful Kingdom**

Jesus Christ proclaimed the kingdom of God when He said, "Repent for the kingdom of God has arrived." His kingdom is not a powerless kingdom; it is a kingdom full of supernatural power. Its power was evident throughout Jesus' ministry as He overpowered the kingdom of darkness that had oppressed so many people through demonic influences or sickness. The kingdom of darkness is known for imprisoning people through fear, demonic oppression, diseases, spiritual blindness, spiritual death, and barrenness. It manipulates people so they cannot break free from its stronghold. Breaking the power or strongholds of the evil forces of this world requires the supernatural power and authority of God. Jesus could set people free because He and His kingdom message were marked by the power and anointing of God. The great news for us, as believers in Christ, is that God has given us the same power that was in Christ so that we too can walk in freedom from oppression and bring freedom to others as well. But sadly, many of us do not realize what kind of power we have as part of the powerful kingdom of God.

The Jesus we have in us is not a weak Jesus or a powerless king. He is the all-powerful King of kings and Lord of lords. He can do great things in and with our lives. He came to earth not only to set people free from the power of the kingdom of darkness but also to delegate the same power of God that was in Him to all His disciples so they could continue expanding and advancing His kingdom to the ends of the earth. If you are part of God's kingdom, then you have been immersed in the anointing of God. In God, you are not weak but strong. You are not poor but rich. You are not hopeless but have hope. And you are not powerless but have the abilities of God and can be used by Him as a blessing and a channel through whom His healing power can be manifested. You are not just an ordinary person—you have been transformed into an extraordinary child of God!

In Luke 10:19–20 Jesus said, "Behold, I have given you authority to tread on serpents and on scorpions, and over all the power of the enemy, and nothing shall hurt you. Nevertheless, do not rejoice in this, that the spirits are subject to you but rejoice that your names are written in heaven" (ESV). Serpents (snakes) and scorpions here symbolize Satan. Just as snakes and scorpions swiftly strike at their prey, so Satan strikes quickly at God's people. But the game changer for us as Jesus' disciples is the power and authority Jesus has given us to tread on the head of Satan. Satan will not hurt us because he is now under our kingdom authority and power. Nevertheless, we are not to rejoice that Satan and his evil spirits are subject to us but rather rejoice that our names are written in heaven.

As we discover the power of God in us, we must not think of ourselves more highly than we ought but rather understand the purpose of God's power in us. The purpose of the power of God in us is not for bragging rights, for dominating others, or for manipulating people for our own gain; rather, it is for us to advance the kingdom of God and bring glory and honor to Him. It is crucial we understand this—otherwise we can abuse the power and authority God has graciously placed upon us and even lead other people away from God. Too many people abuse the anointing of God on their life because they do not understand why God has given them power or spiritual gifts. As you discover and recover the power of God in you, use it to bless people.

**"I Bestow on You a Kingdom"**

At the heart of Jesus' teaching is the kingdom of God and its power, or authority. Mark and Luke both use "kingdom of God" in their Gospels, while Matthew uses "kingdom of heaven." Both expressions mean the same thing. The kingdom of heaven and the kingdom of God are not two different realities. For more on this, I recommend my book *The Parables of the Kingdom*. In that book I extensively explain why Matthew says, "kingdom of heaven" and both Mark and Luke say, "kingdom of God." In this book you will find that sometimes I say "kingdom of God" and sometimes "kingdom of heaven," but both refer to the one and only kingdom that Jesus Christ proclaimed and bestowed on us, His disciples. The kingdom of God is upon us; it is here to empower us to do the will of God and to demonstrate the love, grace, and mercy of God to the oppressed.

Not only did Jesus preach about the kingdom of God and demonstrate its power or jurisdiction over the kingdom of darkness but He also bestowed the kingdom of God upon His disciples. In Luke 22:29 Jesus stated to His disciples, "I bestow on you a kingdom, just as My Father bestowed one on me" (HSCB). This verse sheds more light on who we are and what we have in God as disciples of His Son, Jesus Christ. What does "I bestow on you a kingdom" mean? First, we need to understand that the kingdom of God is not like an earthly kingdom, and it is not a faraway and unreachable place. The kingdom of God is near, and it is reachable because it is rule and reign over people. In simplest terms, "I bestow on you a kingdom" means that just as God bestowed His kingdom power, authority, and reign upon Jesus Christ, so He has also extended His rule and reign to us, Jesus' disciples. He did this so we would proclaim the message of God's kingdom, which is the only message with the power to release people from the kingdom of darkness. No other message has the authority, capability, or power to set people free and sanctify them for God's use. We are no longer useless or ordinary; we are useful and extraordinary because of the power of God in us.

Revelation 5:10 echoes Jesus' words "I bestow on you a kingdom." It states, "You have made them to be a kingdom and priests to serve our God, and they will reign on the earth." In 1 Peter 2:9 we see a similar idea emphasized: "But you are a chosen race, a royal priesthood, a holy nation, a people for His possession, so that you may proclaim the praises of the one who called you out of darkness into His marvellous light." And finally, in Revelation 1:5–6 we are reminded by the Word of God that the blood of Jesus Christ has set us free from our sins and Jesus Himself has made us a kingdom and priests to His God. What we must understand here is that we are not just kingdom in name that lacks power; we are a kingdom with power. The power of the kingdom we now have gives us the privilege of offering spiritual sacrifice to God (worship and praise) as priests and above all else allows us to walk and live in the ever-reigning power of God.

To flow with the power of God, you need to understand you are not an ordinary, weak, hopeless, lifeless, powerless person. You are an extraordinary person who has been infused with the power of heaven. I encourage you to stop living as though you are a weak or powerless Christian who has no future. You are a strong and a mighty man or woman of valor, called and anointed by God to make a difference in the world. You are not just a number in the kingdom of God, waiting to go to heaven someday; you are part of the "now" mission of God.

Today as you read this book as well as the Bible, open your heart to God. Today God wants to do something new in you and revive your passion for the things of God. Today God want to heal you, restore you, give you victory, and transform your life so you can reflect His glory. It is encouraging, uplifting, and empowering to discover that God has dispensed His royal powers to every believer in Christ just as He granted royal powers to His Son, Jesus Christ (Luke 22:29). With His anointing we can and will flourish in His presence here on earth.

The royal powers in Jesus Christ allowed Him to perform many miracles during His ministry, miracles that astounded the religious people and leaders of His day. When He spoke or taught, He did so with authority, power, and wisdom from heaven—not from earth. Those who heard him speak were amazed (Matthew 7:29; Mark 1:22; Luke 4:32). No power could match Jesus' power. His power restored sight to the blind, drove demons away, raised the dead to life, and healed diseases. This is the same power that is on all of us who believe in Christ. The problem is that some of us don't know how to activate it.

The power of God in you cannot be activated unless you have a deeply intimate relationship with Christ and faithful dedication and devotion to God and to His Holy Spirit. For this to happen, you need to unplug from the things of this world and its influences and plug into the kingdom of God through worship, praise, and the Word of God. This will result in a surge of God's power in you. With the power of God working in you, you will be able to move from living in defeat to living in victory.

If we are not walking in the supernatural power of God, we cannot rise up in God's power and fulfill our kingdom mission. It is impossible to set the captives free from the forces of darkness or destroy spiritual strongholds that bind and oppress people. No one can be freed from the influences of the kingdom of darkness by our good sermons preached from our own knowledge or human strength or with a religious spirit. It takes the power of the kingdom of God to break and destroy the yoke of bondage that enslaves people and nations through the influences of the evil forces of darkness.

**The Kingdom of God Is Not a Matter of Talk but of Power**

Paul wrote, "For the kingdom of God is not a matter of talk but of power" (1 Corinthians 4:20). It is crucial for all believers in Christ to understand that the kingdom of God that Jesus Christ introduced and proclaimed was neither a powerless kingdom nor an ordinary kingdom. It was and is an extraordinary kingdom full of divine power. It is not just a matter of talk but is full of action. It exerts power over sickness, infirmities, sin, death, and the forces of darkness.

Paul made sure the people he ministered to understood that the kingdom of God was not a matter of prideful talk but of power. Religious people often are good at talking but lack God's substantial power to walk in love or demonstrate the nature of God. This was the problem of the religious people in Corinth. They had become inflated with pride, and their teaching had no power to bring salvation or freedom to those they preached to. Consequently, Paul examined their teaching from the standpoint of power, not talk. Talk is cheap. A person can easily say, "I will do this or that for the kingdom of God" but too often they lack the power to actually do it. It takes the power of God to teach with substance and produce the intended kingdom results. Religiosity alone cannot bring spiritual or physical transformation. We can teach or preach the Word of God "religiously" yet fail to impact lives for Jesus Christ. Religion cannot change people's lives; only the power of God can do that.

We can know a lot of facts about God, but without the power of God, our words cannot bring deliverance to those who are bound in chains of demonic influence. God's power is effectively revealed through humble servants of God who are devoted to following Jesus Christ and dedicated to His kingdom—not through prideful religious people. A proud religious spirit leads to prideful behavior, empty talk, fake visions, and false prophecies, while humility leads to devotion, dedication, and deep fellowship with God. *God does not measure our spirituality by the knowledge we have of Him but rather by our humility in allowing His Spirit to influence us so we can be and do what His Word says.* The true standard for all of us who have been redeemed by the power of God should never be our "Christianized" eloquent talk but the manifestation of the power of God in and through us. We need the power of God because Satan is not afraid of our polished talk or our knowledge about the kingdom of God or the Word of God. However, Satan is extremely afraid of us if we are walking in the power of the Holy Spirit and actively doing what the Word of God says.

Again, in the kingdom of God talking alone does not produce transformation or bring change—action does. And we act through the power of the Holy Spirit. Thankfully, that power is available to us. Jesus said to His disciples in Luke 24:49, "I am going to send you what my Father has promised [the Holy Spirit]; but stay in the city until you have been clothed with power from on high" (NIV). By sending them the Holy Spirit, Jesus ensured the disciples would be clothed—empowered and endued—with power from heaven so they could put into action all He had taught them to do. The power from heaven was going to empower the disciples to walk in the footsteps of Jesus Christ and proclaim the good news of the kingdom.

Everything supernatural in the kingdom of God is done through the power of the Holy Spirit; therefore, when we discover the Holy Spirit, we discover the very power of God. In Zechariah 4:6 God told Zerubbabel that the rebuilding of the temple was going to be finished but "not by might nor by power, but by God's Spirit." By the Spirit of God we can be what God created us to be and we can do what God has called us to do for Him here on earth.

By God's Spirit we have dominion over the kingdom of darkness and authority over all the schemes of the enemy. The kingdom of God is a kingdom filled with supernatural powers and miracles because the breath and Spirit of God saturate it. If you are born again, you belong to the kingdom of God. And if you belong to the kingdom of God, God has bestowed upon you His kingship. And if you are a king in the kingdom of God, then you have power, authority, and dominion through the Spirit of God over the kingdom of darkness. There are three ways to tell that you are a true king in the kingdom of God, having the Spirit of God and the power of God in you: You will (1) love God with all your heart, (2) easily walk in forgiveness, and (3) love other people. The evidence of the power and Spirit of God in you is not long and impressive prayers, speaking in tongues, or prophetic revelations. The evidence of God's power and Spirit in you is loving God, loving people, and walking in compassion and mercy as Jesus did.

If I speak in the tongues of men and of angels, but have not love, I am only a ringing gong or a clanging cymbal. If I have the gift of prophecy and can fathom all mysteries and all knowledge, and if I have absolute faith so as to move mountains, but have not love, I am nothing. If I give all I possess to the poor and exult in the surrender of my body, but have not love, I gain nothing. (1 Corinthians 13:1–4)

In our own strength, we cannot walk in love or demonstrate the character of God or the kingship He has bestowed upon us. We need the power and Spirit of God. The Spirit of God in us testifies that we are children of the Most High God because we are able not only to walk in the supernatural but also to walk in love, forgiveness, and mercy. We know we have power and anointing from God when we can love others the way God loves us. If we cannot do for others what Christ has done for us—for example, if we can't forgive others—then we are just religious people who lack the Spirit and life of Christ in us. As followers of Jesus Christ, if we can't forgive or love other people, then we are merely religious. Without the breath of God (the Holy Spirit) in us, we are spiritually dead and cannot love, forgive, show mercy, or demonstrate the power of God. A religious spirit in us stops the power of God from being demonstrated. God is more than capable of doing miraculous things in the world today, but religious people who are full of the spirit of familiarity with God are stopping Him from moving. If we look at Jesus' ministry, we see that religious people and leaders were the ones who hindered God from moving mightily in Jesus' hometown. Two thousand years later, the same spirit is still at work, keeping people from walking in the power of God or even understanding they have the power of God in them.

## A Religious Spirit Equals an Empty and Powerless Life and Ministry

A religious spirit is at the top of the list of things that stop people from walking in the power and character of God and demonstrating the true kingdom nature of God. A religious spirit is simply a demonically influenced spirit that pretends to be for God and His kingdom. It is talking good kingdom talk but deep down having no roots, fellowship with God, or connection to Him to understand His will, plan, and purpose.

The tricky part about a religious spirit is that it deceives people by giving them a false understanding of how God moves or wants to do things in the world today, based on their knowledge or studies or cultural background. Consequently, if God tries to move differently or contrary to their beliefs, they do everything possible to try to stop Him. But no one can stop God. He is too powerful. Neither man nor demon can stop God's purpose—His will, purpose, and plan always prevail (Job 42:2). The religious leaders of Jesus' day known as the Pharisees tried to stop Jesus' mission, but they couldn't because God's power was with and in Him. Even those who crucified Him only helped Him accomplish what God had sent Him to do. The point is that a religious spirit stops or hinders God from moving powerfully in our lives and in the nations. It is dangerous to think we know God and all His ways so well that we cannot fathom Him doing something new and fresh from His Spirit.

Let me emphasize here that it is dangerous to be religious and yet lack the Spirit and power of God in our lives. A religious spirit is dangerous because it blinds people to the truth and to the will and vision of God. Furthermore, a religious spirit disables the power of God in the lives of people and in the assembly of God. It paralyzes people from connecting with God and other people heart-to-heart and spirit-to-spirit. A religious spirit can lead us into a sense of familiarity with God, and when we are feel overly familiar with God, our sensitivity to the moving of the Holy Spirit dies. Thus, our own voices become louder than God's voice, and we can't hear God or show mercy to other people. We become judgmental, ministry-position oriented, and critical of other believers' walk with God. We have no passion or desire to see God move in our lives, the lives of others, or in the community. Furthermore, we find ourselves opposing everything and everyone God wants to use for His glory. Our lives become spiritually empty with no substance at all.

If we want to walk in the power of God and impact the kingdom of God, we must first empty ourselves of our proud, fleshly knowledge, wisdom, and understanding and allow the Holy Spirit to impute to us the will, purpose, and plan of God.

Jesus came to show humanity the way out of the power of sin and death through the supernatural power of God. God's kingdom is not about talk but about power—power to free people from the kingdom of darkness and bring them into the kingdom of light and empower them to live for God and do His work. God did not save us to be religious but to have new life in Him and a tender heart like His so that through us He can be seen, appreciated, and glorified. All authority and power both in heaven and on earth belong to Jesus (Matthew 28:18). Thus, for us to have the power of the kingdom of God, we need to turn our lives back to Jesus Christ and abide in Him.

When we discover the supernatural power of God in our lives, our attitude changes. We move from talking about, or even crying out for, revival to becoming revived ourselves. We move from talking about winning souls for the kingdom of God to actually going out and winning souls for Jesus Christ by proclaiming His gospel.

**Walking in the Supernatural Power of God**

The secret to walking in the supernatural power of God lies in being deeply connected to the true Vine, Jesus Christ, and not to the worldly culture and human traditions or systems. In John 15:4 Jesus said, "Remain in Me, and I in you. Just as a branch is unable to produce fruit by itself unless it remains on the vine, so neither can you unless you remain in me." *Remain in Me*. What do those words mean? Jesus was not simply telling His disciples they were to believe in Him, even though that was crucial. He was telling them to abide in Him, meaning to *comply* with His teaching, *obey* it, and *hold on to* it by having their thoughts, emotions, and intentions in union with His. Jesus would also remain in them, meaning they could accomplish anything with His power and presence in them. If the disciples remained in Him and He in them, they would have dynamic power to bear much fruit. But if they didn't remain in Him and He was not with them, they would be fruitless and powerless. They would be cast out, gathered, and burned. By abiding and yielding our lives to the Holy Spirit, we make room for Him to work on our behalf and do things through us that we would never be able to do in our own strength or ability.

Abiding in Jesus Christ is the key to discovering the mysteries of God's kingdom and walking in the supernatural power of God. If we abide in Him, no enemy can destroy us or lead us away from God's purposeful plan for our life. Abiding in Jesus Christ requires our fellowship with and total dedication and connection to the Spirit of God. When we are connected to the Spirit of God, no weapon formed against us can prosper. Furthermore, abiding in Jesus Christ requires us to make Him number one in our lives. If He is not the center of our lives, then it becomes difficult to connect to His power and walk in His tangible presence.

Make Jesus number one today, just as He has made you His number-one treasure and priority. He has a unique plan for you. He doesn't want to make you religious. He wants to make you His disciple and walk with you through the power of His Spirit so you can demonstrate the heart of His Father in heaven to the nations.

God's plans and desires for us can be very different from our own, so we must always do our best to align ourselves to God by uniting our thoughts, intentions, will, and desires with His. It is in Him alone that we can do exploits for the kingdom of God. When we are in union and fellowship with Him, we begin to do great things and bear spiritual fruit. Kingdom power fuels kingdom authority, and kingdom authority lights up a passion for the things of God and motivates us to do good works. Many people today have forgotten that as Christians, our power to heal the sick or set the captives free from the influences of the kingdom of darkness does not come from some kind of holy water, holy cloth, or holy stones but from Yahweh Himself. Healing and deliverance flow from God and not from magic. If you desire God's power, anointing, and Spirit, then you must turn to God Himself and establish a strong fellowship and relationship with Him. Yes, people who are anointed by God can pray for you to receive healing, but healing comes from God alone. God has graciously chosen to manifest His power to heal the sick through human beings, but we must be careful not to worship man for the signs and wonders of God. All praise, glory, and honor belong to God alone.

No program or formula can give us the power of God or victory in life. The only way to walk in God's supernatural power and victory is to remain in Jesus Christ and abide in His Word. In John 15:7 Jesus said, "If you remain in Me and My words remain in you, ask whatever you want and it will be done for you." When Jesus and His words are in you and are the foundation of your life, you can ask anything and it will be done for you. You can command your sickness, weakness, or stumbling blocks to go in the name of Jesus Christ, and they will go because God's power is in you. Through Christ you are now in union with God, His Son, and His Holy Spirit. Because you are in union with the Godhead, the power of the government of heaven is also in you. The power of God in us can be fanned into flames by associating ourselves with God, with His Holy Spirit, and with His Son, Jesus Christ.

## True Anointing Comes from God

In Acts 10:38 Peter revealed the source of the power to do miracles: "God anointed Jesus of Nazareth with the Holy Spirit and with power. Then Jesus went around doing good and healing all who were oppressed by the devil, for God was with Him." The source of Jesus' supernatural power was God the Father. God anointed Jesus and empowered Him with His Holy Spirit to carry out His assignment of redeeming humanity from the kingdom of darkness. Today some people around the world who are desperate for power are turning to satanic spirits for power to perform signs and wonders. In the process they end up bound by evil spirits. Any power that does not come from God cannot bring freedom or prosperity but rather puts people under bondage, spiritual blindness, spiritual death, and torment. Only the power of Jesus Christ can bring true freedom, restoration, and spiritual transformation.

In Matthew 4 we see that immediately after Jesus was empowered by the Holy Spirit from heaven, He was led into the wilderness by the same Holy Spirit to be tempted. It was as if God were saying to the enemy's camp, "Test my Son and see what kind of power He has, for it is not the power from this world but from heaven." The temptation of Jesus Christ in the wilderness by Satan reflects the test the Israelites had faced for forty years in the wilderness. Deuteronomy 8:2–3 says that the Lord led Israel into the wilderness to be tested, but Israel failed its tests. However, Jesus passed His test, and in doing so He established a foundation upon which mankind could continue to have victory over the kingdom of darkness. To this day, victory over the forces of evil can be achieved only through the power of the name of Jesus Christ. Therefore, the Bible instructs us to pray or ask anything in the name of Jesus Christ, and God will grant our request (see John 14:13–14; 15:16; 16:24; 1 John 5:14).

In our next chapter we will look in greater detail at the power of the name of Jesus. His name has the power, dominion, and authority to establish or reestablish anything the enemy has destroyed or stolen. Praying in the name of Jesus is simply aligning ourselves with the power and authority the name of Jesus carries.

Philippians 2:10 says, "At the name of Jesus every knee should bow, in heaven and on earth and under the earth." It is through the name of Jesus Christ that we receive our salvation, live, and have our dominion. Thus, whatever we bind on earth will be bound in heaven, and whatever we loose on earth will be loosed in heaven (Matthew 18:18).

Jesus overcame temptations because He walked in the power of the Holy Spirit. I think it is safe for us to say that the Israelites could not pass their test in the wilderness because God had not yet released the power of His Holy Spirit to dwell in them—even though we see Him at work among them. Consequently, God promised in several places to give them a new heart and a new Spirit (Ezekiel 11:19; 36:26; Jeremiah 31:33; Deuteronomy 30:6). With a new heart empowered by the Holy Spirit, God's people would not only obey God's instructions but also walk in the power of His Word, or instructions. Jesus overcame temptation in the wilderness and emerged victorious after forty days of testing because He was immersed in the power of the Holy Spirit.

When Jesus was about to go to His Father, He instructed His disciples to wait in the city until they had been clothed with the heavenly power of the Holy Spirit (Luke 24:49). The reason for this is clear: without the power of the Holy Spirit, they could not carry out their mission of advancing God's kingdom or live their lives according to God's will and purpose. It is sad that today many people want to advance the kingdom of God by mixing the power of God with the spirit of this world (flesh, carnality). Flesh gives birth to flesh (carnality), and carnality is characterized by unspiritual tendencies and attitudes. Carnality opens us to the influences of the world, which makes us spiritually weak and powerless (though often religious). Living life according to the Word of God and in the power of the Spirit of God makes us strong in the Lord, stable and unshakable in our faith. Jesus was unshakable during Satan's testing because He lived His life here on earth not according to the standards of this world but according to the will of His Father in heaven. Everywhere He ministered He demonstrated the rule and reign of God. He healed the sick, restored the sight of the blind, and made the lame walk again because that was the will of God the Father.

## Jesus' Power and Authority Demonstrated

Throughout Jesus' ministry, He demonstrated the rule and reign of God by healing the sick and commanding authority over demonic influences. In Luke 4:35 we are told that Jesus rebuked the demon. "'Be silent!' He said. 'Come out of him!' Then the demon threw the man down before them all and came out without harming him." His words had divine authority, and no demon could resist coming out of a person. The people of Jesus' day who witnessed His amazing kingdom powers in Capernaum were astounded. In Luke 4:36 we are told that all the people were overcome with amazement and asked one another, "What is this word? For with authority and power he commands the unclean spirits, and they come out!"

It's interesting that Jesus did not engage in a ritual-like tradition to cast the demon out of the person. All He did was simply rebuke the unclean spirit, and the spirit came out. What does that show us? It shows us the magnitude of the power of the kingdom of God that was and is in Him. Right after rebuking the unclean spirit and casting it out of the man, Jesus entered Simon's house. Simon's mother-in-law was suffering from a high fever, and they asked Jesus about her. So He stood over her and rebuked the fever, and it left her. She got up immediately and began to serve them (Luke 4:38–39). Scripture after scripture in the Gospels show us Jesus healing people through the power of the kingdom of God. Any foreign gods the people looked up to for healing could not match Jesus' power or authority. Some Pharisees (religious folks) even accused Him of using the power of Beelzebul, the prince of the demons, to drive out the demons because they could not comprehend the power and authority flowing out of Him and would not attribute them to God. Jesus responded by stating this:

> Every kingdom divided against itself is headed for destruction, and no city or house divided against itself will stand. If Satan drives out Satan, he is divided against himself, how then will his kingdom stand? If I drive out demons by Beelzebul, who is it your sons drive them out by? For this reason they will be your judge. If I drive out demons by the Spirit of God, then the kingdom of God has come to you. (Matthew 12:24–28)

Who was Beelzebul? Beelzebul is believed to be an ancient name for Baal, a Canaanite storm or fertility god. Baal was a pagan god, and in the ancient world demonic spirits were at work in the pagan religions (see Psalm 106:28, 36–39; 1 Corinthians 10:19–20). Satan himself was the spirit at work in Baal worship; therefore, the name *Beelzebub* became strongly connected to or an alternate name for Satan. The Pharisees apparently believed Beelzebul had power over unclean spirits because he was the god of unclean spirits. Therefore, they were accusing Jesus of using the powers of Satan to deliver people from Satan, which doesn't make sense at all. Jesus reminded them that Satan could not undermine his own kingdom and work against himself because a kingdom divided against itself is doomed for destruction. In other words, Satan cannot cast out Satan because evil plus evil equals evil—not good. No evil can bring freedom, redemption, or victory over unclean spirits because evil produces unclean spirits and enslaves people. It always brings destruction.

When Jesus said, "If I drive out demons by the Spirit of God, then the kingdom of God has come to you," He was informing the Pharisees, as well as any who looked to pagan gods for spiritual and physical restoration, that the rule and reign of the kingdom of God, which truly sets people free, had arrived. His emphasis was on the words "the kingdom of God has come," which meant that the kingdom of God to which many people looked to bring freedom and restoration had arrived sooner than they expected. What were the signs of its arrival? Demons were being forced to release people from their captivity, and those afflicted by sickness were being healed. The power of the kingdom of God is the only power that silences the kingdom of darkness. Satan seduces people by giving them false and temporal things such as money or good fortune but with a hidden agenda of destroying their lives. Be careful to give your life only to Jesus Christ.

## Jesus Demonstrated God's Power in His Teaching

Jesus demonstrated power and authority through His teaching. His teachings were so powerful and full of kingdom authority that the religious leaders of His day were shocked. His messages came directly from God and not from the traditions of the religious authorities or leaders of earlier generations whom Jewish teachers generally cited. As Christians and ministers of the gospel, we must realize it is impossible to walk in the supernatural and see God's signs and wonders without being connected to the Spirit of God. Moreover, we cannot demonstrate the pure heart of God in our preaching or teaching by getting our message or sermons from other preachers, Google, current news, or what we hear or see happening around us or in the lives of others. The source of our message must be Jesus Christ and the Holy Spirit because it is when we preach, teach, or minister from the power of the Holy Spirit and from the heart of

Jesus Christ that things happen both in our lives and in the lives of those we minister to. If we desire to make an impact for God in the world today, we must desire to imitate Jesus Christ and preach the message He preached—the kingdom message. If you preach any other gospel, you will never make a true impact for God in the lives of people.

As a minister I have discovered that preaching the problem only results in more problems or a hard heart. But preaching Jesus, the solution, results in a soft heart, which leads to transformation. Jesus preached the solution to the problem of sin, and as a result our lives have been transformed. I am not saying we cannot point out the problem, but when we focus on the solution to the problem, deliverance flows swiftly. Conversely, when we magnify or put too much emphasis on the problem, it becomes a stumbling block to transformation. It is time to call for repentance because we have the solution. Sin has condemned us already; consequently, we need the good news of Jesus Christ to offer us a way out of its chains, and the Word of God to continually overcome its power.

The power to set captives free from unclean spirits or influences comes by preaching the gospel of Jesus Christ alone. It doesn't come from our eloquent speech, theological knowledge, titles or positions in ministry, or any set of rules. Jesus is still the deliverer and the life changer. Through Him alone we too can be channels through whom people experience life transformation and are empowered to live for the kingdom of God. All power, authority, and anointing to do the work of God, to live for Jesus Christ, and to impact the world come by being disciples of Jesus Christ, which in turn requires several things:

- Dwelling in the presence of God
- Meditating on the Word of God
- Fellowshipping with God and other believers

- Having faith and trust in God's ability
- Walking in the Spirit and allowing Him to influence our lives
- Accepting the rule and reign of God
- Having the mind of Christ, not the mind of the world
- Devoting our lives to Jesus Christ

It is unfortunate that so many of us say we want to see the power of God at work in our lives, in the lives of others, and in our nations, but we are not willing to spend time in the presence of God through prayer and studying of God's Word or to step out to do the work of God. We have time for everything else but no time to seek Jesus Christ. The only time we seek Him is when we are in trouble or need Him to do something for us.

God is not a vending machine; He desires the time and fellowship of His children. Jesus said, "Seek first his kingdom and His righteousness, and all these things will be given to you as well" (Matthew 6:33). If we value the reign of God on our lives through the Holy Spirit, then we will diligently seek and pursue God and allow Him to use us mightily. It is when we are in the presence of the anointed King of kings, Jesus Christ, that God reveals and imparts His power and anointing to us. Furthermore, in His presence we can hear God's voice, receive spiritual direction, be convicted of our shortcomings, and be empowered to turn away from the ways of the world and toward the ways of God.

When you are in the presence of the King, God's vision for your life is illuminated, and the path to your kingdom destiny is cleared for you to travel without fear. Your destiny and future in life are achieved by dwelling continually in the shadow of the almighty God.

## When You Are Saturated by the Holy Spirit, Your Focus Shifts to Kingdom Business

> So when they came together, they asked Him, "Lord will You at this time restore the kingdom to Israel?" Jesus replied, "It is not for you to know times or seasons that the Father has fixed by His own authority. But you will receive power when the Holy Spirit comes upon you, and you will be My witnesses in Jerusalem, and in all Judea and Samaria, and to the ends of the earth." (Acts 1:6–8)

Even after Jesus' resurrection, the disciples seemed to be consumed with wanting to know when the end would come and when Jesus would restore the kingdom to Israel. Their focus clearly was not aligned with Jesus'. The first-century Jews longed for the restoration of the kingdom of Israel, and they believed the Messiah, who would come from David's roots, would accomplish this mission. The disciples also longed for the kingdom, especially now that the Messiah they had anticipated had finally arrived. They missed the point here because they were focused on a physical kingdom while Jesus was focused on a spiritual kingdom. Jesus was concerned with making a spiritual impact on their lives and in the lives of others, not a military impact. His heart was for them to be His witnesses in Jerusalem, in Judea and Samaria, and beyond. Only after that mission of proclaiming His good news is accomplished will the end come (Matthew 24:14). Jesus instructed them to wait in the city for His Spirit to be poured out upon them. In Acts 2 this promise was fulfilled when the Holy Spirit came. But what is so intriguing is that immediately after the Holy Spirit was poured out upon them, they went out and preached the good news of Jesus Christ and urged people to repent of their sin and turn to Jesus Christ, the only solution to sin. About three thousand people accepted their message in one day and were baptized and added to the family of God (Acts 2:41).

The promise that the disciples would receive power when the Holy Spirit had come upon them was a great promise that God fulfilled. The disciples needed the power of the Holy Spirit to shift their focus from a physical, worldly kingdom to a spiritual, godly kingdom. When the Holy Spirit had come upon them, He empowered them to focus on what their master, Jesus Christ, was and is focused on—souls. Jesus was passionate about winning lost souls and bringing them into the kingdom of God. The Holy Spirit was the power in the disciples that drew many to the message they preached and eventually to God. This shows us that through the Holy Spirit, we have power to win souls for the kingdom of God and to bring restoration to our broken world. You may ask, "How can I discover or rediscover the power of God in my life?" The answer is simple and straightforward: turn to the Holy Spirit. He is already living in you if you are born again. If you are not born again, the power of God is not available to you. You first need to surrender your life to Jesus Christ.

If you are born again and yet are not walking in the power of God, check your connection and fellowship with the Holy Spirit. If you connect to Him today, you will activate or reactivate His power, authority, and anointing in your life. Your focus will shift from the carnal to the spiritual, and your passion for Jesus Christ and zeal for the Word of God will increase in all aspects of your life. Above all, you will be able to flow with the Holy Spirit as He flows and speak His word as He inspires you.

For the church to forcefully advance the kingdom of God here on earth and demonstrate its rule and reign, it needs the power of the kingdom of God and His authority. Only the power and authority of God's kingdom can transform the hurting world. May the Holy

Spirit saturate Christ's church once again and awaken our spirit to Him so we can have a kingdom mind-set, attitude, and passion and a heart for the things Jesus cares about. May He change our lives, not so we can feel good about ourselves but so He can work through us. Lord, cleanse us from the religious spirit that has kept Your church in bondage and blocked us from walking in Your rule and reign. Send Your fire to purify, sanctify, and wash us from the spirit of the world, and awaken us to Your vision, Your will, and Your ways so we can do what You have called us to do for Your kingdom!

## We Discover the Power of God by Walking in the Spirit, Not in the Flesh

Two kingdoms influence the world: the kingdom of God (light) and the kingdom of Satan (darkness). It is apparent the kingdom of darkness has a powerful influence on today's world, as evidenced by such evils as murder, hatred for one another, and division both in the nations and in the church. Satan's goal for his kingdom of darkness is to destabilize the plan God has for His created people and divide God's people so they cannot function in His power. Evil takes root where carnality is dominant. Where carnality rules, the Spirit of God is absent; thus, strife, hatred, fighting, division, lawlessness, and unrighteous acts prevail. We cannot walk in the flesh and in the Spirit of God at the same time—there is no in-between. If we are walking in the Spirit, the influence of the Spirit of God will be evident in our lives; if we are walking in the flesh, its influence will affect our actions toward one another and toward God. Sadly, many Christians are not walking in the power of God because the flesh is dominating their lives.

> For you were called to be free, brothers; only don't use this freedom as an opportunity for the flesh, but serve one another through love. For the entire law

> is fulfilled in one statement: Love your neighbor as yourself. But if you bite and devour one another, watch out, or you will be consumed by one another. I say then walk by the Spirit and you will not carry out the desires of the flesh. (Galatians 5:13–16)

The ungodly behavior exhibited by some of the Galatians Paul was addressing originated from the influence of the flesh. To correct that, Paul encouraged them to walk by the Spirit and not by their flesh. Many things in our lives and in the body of Christ can be fixed if we reject our fleshly desires and humbly submit to the Spirit of God. When the kingdom of God is in us, we begin to see people as God sees them and love our neighbors as we love ourselves. Then the dissensions in our midst disappear. When we walk in the Spirit of God, we discover the power to show mercy and forgive and to love and embrace other people and work with them in unity. When a person is influenced, or possessed, by the kingdom of God, that person does good deeds on behalf of the King of the kingdom, Jesus Christ. The opposite is true as well: when a person is influenced by the kingdom of darkness, he or she does bad deeds on behalf of the kingdom of the devil.

The Bible is full of great examples of people who were influenced by the power of the Holy Spirit and did good things for the kingdom of God. Jesus Christ, of course, is the greatest example of that. He was anointed "with the Holy Spirit and power, and he went around doing good and healing all who were under the power of the devil, because God was with him" (Acts 10:38).

When you walk according to the Holy Spirit living in you, you will do good deeds of the kingdom and demonstrate the heart of God to other people. Allow the kingdom of God to influence your mind, tongue, and spirit so you can display the glory of God and reflect His tender heart.

## You Have the Prevailing Strength and Power of God in You

Here is what Job had to say about the majestic power of God: "If it is a matter of strength, look, He is the Mighty One!" (Job 9:19). The Hebrew word for *strength* here signifies a prevailing strength or a conquering strength. God's dynamic power is all conquering and triumphant over death, sickness, sin, unfruitfulness, and any spiritual powers of this world. It must be emphasized here that God not only *has* dynamic "power" (*dunamis*), but power *is* His character and nature. When God's children are open to the influence of His rule and reign, they too have the prevailing strength, abilities, and power of His Spirit. Moreover, their strength is in the name of Jesus Christ, and in Him they live, breathe, and have their being. No evil can destroy them because Jesus Christ, the firm foundation, anchors their lives.

In these perilous times it is more critical than ever before to understand that without the power of God it is impossible to advance the kingdom of God by setting the captives free ... proclaiming the gospel of Jesus Christ effectively in a hostile environment ... fulfilling our kingdom callings ... stepping out in faith to do the will of God ... living fearless and Christ-like lives ... using our kingdom gifts to help the body of Christ ... and working with other men and women of God to build the body of Christ. Trying to live our lives for Jesus Christ through the lenses of our own religious understanding or reasoning or strength leads to disappointment and spiritual unfruitfulness. In 1 Corinthians 2:5 Paul said, "My message and my preaching were not in persuasive words of wisdom, but in the demonstration of the Spirit and power, so that your faith would not rest on the wisdom of men, but on the power of God." We can talk religiously, but what matters at the end of the day is the fruits or results of our talk. Any talk or preaching without the backing of the power of the Holy Spirit cannot bring transformation or healing to a suffering soul.

It's about time we believers in Christ begin to function in the kingdom of God and not just sit idly glued to the pews of the church while people in our communities are perishing. When you have the anointing of God and His divine power and authority working in and through you, it is impossible to live a fruitless life. It's through the dynamic power of God that we can effectively function in the kingdom of God, win souls for His Kingdom, and advance the rule and reign of His kingdom. Furthermore, it's through the power of God that we can demonstrate the character and nature of God.

In our next chapter we will look at the power and authority we have in the name of Jesus Christ. We will discuss how we can use that power and authority to advance the kingdom of God and rise above any obstacles or storms of life and proclaim the good news of the kingdom of God. Through the power of the name of Jesus Christ we can love the unlovable, forgive the unforgivable, and illustrate to the world the compassionate heart of God.

## Chapter 4

# THE POWER OF JESUS' NAME

His Name Is Your Weapon of Spiritual Warfare

Names in the Bible are important. They often paint a bigger picture of the function, calling, or strength of an individual or a group of people. When we examine the names in the Bible, we find that most of them tell a story about the people and the land and about God the creator and His dealings with humanity. In our modern world, names are mostly used for personal identification purposes, but in the Middle Eastern world a name identifies more than just an individual. It gives a clue about the individual's background, character, and nature and about the character of the person's family lineage. In many cultures a name alone can tell which tribe, village, and lineage a person is from. In the Bible we see that most people were named according to their mission or task in life—not after favorite personalities or family members or friends. To know a person's name in the biblical world was to some extent equivalent to knowing the reputation and character of that person and of his or her family.

## The Significance of a Name

In Middle Eastern culture, a person from one tribe or family who wants to marry usually seeks to marry into a family with a good reputation in society so their name will not be tarnished or corrupted. If a family doesn't have a good name or reputation in society, people who associate with that family are considered corrupt and risk destroying their own reputation. And if a family member commits a crime, it affects the name of the family in the community. This echoes Proverbs 22:1: "A good name is more desirable than great riches; to be esteemed is better than silver or gold." Ecclesiastes 7:1 says something similar: "A good name is better than a good ointment."

In Luke 19:1–10 we see something comparable. When Jesus was the guest of a tax collector named Zacchaeus, the crowds were outraged because tax collectors had a very bad name, or reputation. They were considered terrible sinners because they charged more taxes than they were supposed to and kept some of the money for themselves. But Zacchaeus was not only a tax collector; he was the *chief* tax collector and supervised other tax collectors in his district. He enriched himself by taking advantage of his position and extorting money from people. So in the court of public opinion he was a bad guy, a sinner with a bad name. According to the people, a person of Jesus' caliber shouldn't have any contacts or association with such a person.

Jesus, of course, was the Messiah and Savior, and He did not come to save "good" people or associate only with people who had a clean reputation. He came to save people with bad reputations or names (the lost) because of sin. Through His renowned and reputable name, they would find salvation and ultimately a good, clean, and reputable name. But according to the religious people, Jesus should not have gone into the home of such a sinful man as Zacchaeus. To have listened to them, however, would have defeated Jesus' purpose and mission of saving the lost.

Have you been rejected, cast aside, and avoided because of your past by people who see themselves as righteous? Through the name of Jesus Christ you can find acceptance. Just because some super-spiritual people have rejected you doesn't mean Jesus has rejected you or has lost interest in you. You are a great candidate for the grace of God and a new name through Jesus Christ. So turn to Jesus Christ. He will give you a good name and reputation and fix all that concerns you.

## A Good Name Brings Honor to the Family

In the ancient world people's names defined their character and deeds in life and the way they were remembered in death. A family member's actions could either build or destroy the reputation of the family name in the community. Consequently, people in the ancient world lived as groups and not individuals. They honored one another for the sake of the reputation of their families and the God they served and worshipped.

Christians too are called to live and function in a group called "the body of Christ" and not in isolation as individuals. Paul put it very clearly: "If one member suffers, all the members suffer with it; if one member is honored, all members rejoice with it" (1 Corinthians 12:26). In the kingdom of God each kingdom dweller has a place and function. Our conduct is crucial because it can bring either praise or shame to the King of the kingdom (Jesus Christ). Furthermore, if one person is hurting, the entire body of believers will be hurting. If we can grasp this kingdom insight, I believe we will stop gossiping, slandering, and assassinating each other's character because doing so affects all of us as the body of Christ. It also destroys the name of the God we serve or claim to serve. When Christians fight one another, the damage goes beyond our own reputation and into the realm of God's reputation, calling into question His credibility, integrity, and character.

If we have accepted the rule and reign of God on our life (if we have been born again), we represent the government of the kingdom of God. But more than that, we represent the reputation, credibility, integrity, and character of Jesus Christ, who is the Head of the body of Christ and the King of the kingdom of God. Being a disciple of Jesus Christ (a Christian) is a serious matter and must be taken seriously. We are ambassadors of the kingdom of God. Our behavior both in and outside the church can either bring damage to the name of Jesus Christ or bring Him much joy, glory, respect, honor, and praise. People who do not know God draw their impressions of Him from their encounters with us Christians. Our lives give them a picture of the God we serve. If we are mean or rude to people, they will see the God we serve as mean or rude. Therefore, we must be careful not to misrepresent God but to represent Him with the honor and dignity His holy name deserves. Yahweh is not a dictator. He is not rude, arrogant, or unforgiving. He is not hateful or hardhearted. He is tenderhearted, gentle, forgiving, and good to all. Moreover, His names reveal to us His attributes of power, authority, dominion, majesty, and strength. We will look into this more as we go on, but for now let's continue to look at the importance of a name in the Bible and learn more about its remarkable influence. This will help us understand why the name of Jesus Christ is such an influential name and a powerful spiritual weapon against the kingdom of darkness.

## Biblical Definition of *Name*

In the biblical sense, a name has a deeper meaning than just an identifying title. It represents a person's influence and attributes. The

Hebrew word for *name* is *shem*. The Hebraic meaning of the word *shem*, however, goes far beyond our Western cultural understanding of the meaning of a name. In Jewish culture *shem* has a meaning that ranges from "renown," "honor," or "fame," to "report." In the Greek language the word for *name* is *onoma*, which comes from a verb that can sometimes be translated "known." Because of this, a name indicates how a person or object is to be known or is known. With this understanding, it is safe to say that a name gives a report (good or bad) about a person or place. For example, bearing the name of Christ (*Christian*) goes far beyond our religious understanding of the title. Being called a Christian expresses something deep about Christ the Messiah and all He is and desires to be in our lives and in the lives of other people. That is why Ephesians 5:1–9 commands us to imitate Christ—that is, take on His attributes—in everything we do. When we have His mind-set, we can represent His kingdom in ways that reflect His glory and honor. To be a Christian is not to hang a convenient label of Christianity or religion around our neck and show people in the world how evil they are and how good we are; rather, it's to reflect the glory, honor, love, and mercy of Jesus Christ our Messiah and King. Through our testimony of His goodness, we proclaim His renowned name and make it famous in all the earth.

The honorable name of Jesus Christ provides us with a name and reputation in society and a different attitude and lifestyle. Before we were in Christ, we had a bad reputation and were full of darkness. Now the light of the name of Jesus, a name above any other name both here on earth and in the heavens, has shone over our lives, and we have power to live as people of the Light (Jesus Christ) and through His name produce what is good, right, and true. When we are in His name, we are new creations, and we take no part in the worthless deeds of evil. Instead, we expose evil and its deception through the Word of God.

On a side note, don't condemn or judge people who are yet to experience life under the name of Jesus Christ. Rather, do your best to demonstrate how good it is to be in Christ so you can inspire them to desire the same for their lives. Likewise, if you see other believers living outside the renowned name of Jesus Christ, help them, pray for them, and encourage them to turn back to the ways of Christ. Condemnation doesn't help anyone living outside the will of God to turn to Him, but love does. We don't love the sins that may be in a person's life, but we do love the person created by God. Jesus did not love Zacchaeus's sins, but He loved Zacchaeus as a man created by God and deserving an opportunity for the grace and mercy of God. That is why Jesus risked His reputation to go to Zacchaeus's home.

**The Influence of a Good or Bad Name**

In Middle Eastern culture, as well as other cultures around the world, a good or bad name has an influence on society. A bad name will directly or indirectly influence people to do evil deeds, while a good name will in one way or another influence people to do good deeds. If a person or a place is named after an evil spirit, chances are that person or place will be influenced by the same spirit. Many people avoid a bad reputation by all means, while they pursue, praise, and cherish a good name. Satan does anything he can to tarnish Christians' reputations so people will avoid them when they try to present the gospel of Jesus Christ.

How many people have told you to avoid certain places of worship or particular Christians? They may threaten that if you associate with those people, they will consider you to be like them. They may even quote Amos 3:3: "Can two walk together, except they be agreed?" Satan does not change. His tactics to destroy the work of God are always the same. He uses slander to tarnish the believer's character and name in society.

When you have a good reputation and name as a follower of Christ and are proclaiming nothing but His pure gospel, you can influence many for Him. Your reputation should not be established by what you have accomplished in life but in the name above all names, the name of Jesus Christ. If you try to keep your dignity and reputation in the community solely through your works, you will be disappointed, but if you honor the name of God, you will never be put to shame.

The name of Jesus Christ is a great and powerful name, and all those who desire to do the will of God and good deeds for people must do so in His name. It is the only name that can influence us to do mighty things for the kingdom of God, and through it we can advance God's purpose and kingdom plan. Anything done in the name and Spirit of God produces great results and brings freedom to those who are bound in any areas of their lives. Satan and his agents cannot withstand the power of the name of Jesus Christ because Jesus' name is like a light and turns darkness into light.

The name of Jesus Christ is a distinctive mark upon believers, and His name describes to us who Jesus Christ is (God with us) and who we are in Him. Knowing who you are in Christ and what you have through the name of Jesus Christ is very liberating. It can empower you to rise and do what in your own strength or ability you cannot do. The name of God or His Son, Jesus Christ, is not to be taken simply as a label or an arbitrary way of identifying God and His kingdom. In biblical usage and in the spiritual realm, the names of God and Jesus correctly describe God's attributes of power and indicate the essential hallmark or distinction of His influence, glory, majesty, and nature as compared with other so-called gods such as Baal. The names of God simply reveal who God is, by what principles He operates, and what He can do.

*Dr. Kazumba Charles*

## Names Reveal the Character or Nature of a Person

Adam named all the animals (Genesis 2:19–20), apparently giving them names that in some way reflected their nature. In turn, their names became so associated with the animals as to convey certain characteristics themselves. Thus, the name "lion" to this day suggests courage, power, and strength. For this reason some people in the Hebrew culture named their children *Ariel* (Ezra 8:16; cf. 2 Samuel 23:20), which literally means "lion of God." And in Revelation 5:5 Jesus is referred to as the "Lion of the tribe of Judah" because of His majestic power and strength.

Noah and Jesus are two more examples of biblical names that reveal to us something about a person and even his mission. Lamech, Noah's father, named his son Noah, saying, "This one will bring us relief from the agonizing labor of our hands, caused by the ground the Lord has cursed" (Genesis 5:29). Noah's name means "one who brings relief and comfort," and in Genesis 7–8 we see how he obeyed and acted on God's instruction to build the ark and bring relief and comfort. Most of the people did not take him seriously, but because of His actions he brought relief and comfort from the destructive power of the flood to his household and the animal kingdom.

In Matthew 1:20–21 the angel of the Lord appeared to Joseph and told Him, "Mary will give birth to a son, and you are to name Him Jesus [which means "Savior"], because He will save His people from their sins." The name *Jesus* is the Greek form of the Hebrew name *Joshua*, which means "Yahweh saves." Isaiah 7:14 and 8:8 and Matthew 1:23 refer to Jesus as Immanuel, meaning "God with us" or "God is with us." The names Jesus (*Yeshua*) and Immanuel fit the mission, task, and purpose of Jesus Christ on earth as the Savior of His people from sins. The name Immanuel also indicates that God's presence was now coming to dwell among His people. Jesus' names reveal much about His mission. When we look at the life and ministry of Jesus, we see that everything He did lived up to the meaning of His name. He rescued sinners from the punishment of sin, and through Him people experienced salvation and God dwelled among them. His name had not only influence but also power to set the captives free. In Acts 4:12 Peter made this very clear: "There is salvation in no one else, for there is no other name under heaven given to people, and we must be saved by it." There is no salvation in any other name. Neither Buddha, nor Muhammad, nor any other man or man-made god can save people from the power of sin and death. In John 14:6 Jesus stated, "No one comes to the Father except through me."

Jesus is the only way, truth, and life. If you want to know the truth, or find life, or find a way to God the Father, you must turn to Jesus. He alone can provide access to God and His supernatural power. Jesus is the truth (John 1:14, 17; 5:33; 18:37; 8:40, 45–46) and the life (John 1:4). He is more than able to confer eternal life on you and me if we believe in His name (John 3:16). To have Jesus in our life and to live in His name is to live under the power of God. Because Jesus' name is above every other name, in His name we have supernatural power to defeat any satanic forces and agents. Calling on His name is simply calling on the supernatural powers of God. Consequently, we must pray through His powerful name. In Jesus, God has given us a name above every name by which we can fight our enemies and live life. Furthermore, through His name we are new creations. The glory, majestic power, and anointing of Jesus Christ shine on all His disciples and followers. We have no reason to be afraid because in Him we are strong warriors and overcomers. Through the powerful name of Jesus Christ we have been made a new people in union with Him. It's as though we have been given a new name.

*Dr. Kazumba Charles*

## In the Spiritual Realm a New Name Equals a New Position or Influence

Paul wrote, "Therefore, if anyone is in Christ, he is a new creation; old things have passed away, and look, new things have come" (2 Corinthians 5:17). A person who is in Christ is born again, or regenerated, into something new through the power of the name of Jesus Christ and given a new name ("King" and "Priest"). This new name is equivalent to a new position and speaks of a radical change or transformation that takes places in the believer's life.

In the Bible when a person was given a new position or a radical change took place in his life, a new name was given him to indicate his new characteristic. Abraham is a good example of that. His original name was Abram, which means "exalted father," but God changed his name to Abraham, meaning the "father of many" (Genesis 17:5). Abram was elevated to a new position in which he would be extremely fruitful. When he was Abram, he had no children, but as Abraham he would become the father of multitudes.

Another good example of a name change is Jacob. He was the third person in the Bible to be renamed by God—first were Abraham and then Sarah (Genesis 17:5–15). Jacob's name was changed to Israel, "one who strives with God" (Genesis 32:28). This name change came after his wrestling match with the Angel of the Lord (Genesis 32:25–28), when he refused to let the Angel of the Lord go until he blessed Jacob. The other interesting thing in this account is that soon after the Angel had renamed Jacob "Israel," Jacob, or Israel, also renamed Penuel, the place where he fought the Angel of the Lord. The new name was Peniel, meaning "the face of God," because he had seen God face to face and yet had been spared from death. The renaming of Penuel to Peniel gave the place a new and high significance, and it became a memorial of Jacob's face-to-face encounter with God.

These name changes were important because they expressed the most important characteristics of the ones renamed. In simplest terms, if a place was named after an evil figure, the character or spirit of that evil figure would influence the place or occupy it. Now think of this: If a person is named after an evil character, what spirit do you think will influence the person? Names are important. That is why the Bible says God gave Jesus a name above all names, meaning the Spirit and power behind the name of Jesus Christ will rule, influence, and overpower all spirits or powers behind evil names. When you pray "in the name of Jesus," remember that it is not a formula by which God answers your prayers; rather, you are simply appealing to the power and authority in the name of Jesus Christ to take action over your situation or circumstance. Furthermore, when you pray "in the name of Jesus Christ," you are making a powerful statement of assurance. If you command sickness to go in the power and authority of Jesus' name, that sickness will go because you called upon a name that is more powerful than the name "sickness."

**Names Have Power, Authority, and Influence**

Names have a deeper and greater impact, either positive or negative, over people and places than we often understand because a name carries power. When you give a person (including yourself) a name, the spirit or power behind that name, which may be good or bad, goes with it and becomes a major influence upon the person's attitude or character. This is why it's important to give your children or even your place of business names that have a good spirit and influence. Never name them after bad characters. Name them after good characters because what you "name" or "call out" is established. If you name your son "Trouble," the chances of his becoming a troublemaker are high. It is crucial as we look at the power of the name of Jesus Christ to understand that names are powerful; they have either a good or a bad impact on a person. In the spiritual realm a name identifies the origin, influence, or source of the power or spirit of a person or place.

Behind every person's action there is an influencer, and that influencer has a name. It is either the good name of Jesus Christ influencing a person's attitudes, thoughts, and actions or the evil name of Satan. Only two kingdoms wish to reign and rule in the hearts and lives of people here on earth—the kingdom of God and the kingdom of darkness. Our actions, attitudes, and character reveal the governing power of our life. If the name of Jesus Christ is the governing authority of our life, then Jesus' character, goodness, mercy, love, and compassion will be evident in the way we live. To walk in the power of Jesus Christ, we must allow His powerful name to rule our heart, mind, soul, and body. We can't walk in the manifest power of God without standing on the name of Jesus Christ, for there is power in the name of Jesus—power to bring the dead back to life and to do wonders. The name Jesus (*Yeshua*) is not only a beautiful name but also one with authority and power over every other name. Through the name of Jesus the sick are made well, the lost find salvation, sinners receive redemption, and the bound are set free. Through the name of Jesus Christ we can dismantle and destroy the forces of darkness that operate under the evil influence of the name of Satan and his agents.

As believers in Christ, when we discover the power God the Father has infused in the name of Jesus Christ, understand its authority over all other names on earth or in heaven, and continually gravitate toward the tender and yet powerful name of Jesus, no evil can destroy us. Why? Because we live, breathe, and walk under the authoritative name of Jesus Christ. The devil is not afraid of *what* we know, but He is afraid of *whom* we know and *whose* we are. If you know the Lord Jesus Christ as your Lord and Savior and are living according to His Word, then Satan has no business with you. But if you know Jesus Christ but still live by the standards, traditions, or culture of this world, then I can guarantee you Satan and his agents have unfinished business with you. The enemy isn't afraid of what you know about Jesus Christ, but he is afraid when you live your life under the power and anointing of the name of Jesus Christ. In whose name do you fight your spiritual battles or live your life? Do you trust in the name of your skill set, educational background, money, or religious understanding? That is not enough. You can have victory over your life struggles only through the name of Jesus Christ.

As we think further on the power of names, let us turn once again to the story of David and Goliath. First Samuel 17:45 reads, "Then David said to the Philistine, 'You come to me with sword, a spear, and a javelin, but I come to you in the name of the Lord of hosts, the God of the armies of Israel, whom you have taunted.'" By stating, "I come to you in the name of the Lord of hosts, the God of the armies of Israel," David was simply revealing his source of power, strength, and victory, both to Goliath and to the intimidated army of Israel, which for forty days could not step out and challenge the giant Philistine. David's secret weapon against Goliath was the power of the name of God. While Goliath's strength was in his experience as a mighty warrior using his sword, spear, and javelin better than anyone else, no skill—no matter how great—can defeat a person whose power is in the name of God.

In Psalm 20:7 David again made it clear in whose name he fought his battles and gained victory: "Some take pride in chariots, and others in horses, but we take pride in the name of Yahweh our God." The point here is that human strength, skills, talents, and armaments are of no value if God is not with us and fighting for us. Consequently, we are not to take pride in our human abilities but rather rejoice because of the power we have in the name of God our Father. Through His name we can overcome life's challenges. If we trust too much in our abilities, we will fail. If we trust the name of Jesus Christ, we will never be disappointed.

*Dr. Kazumba Charles*

## Names Are Not Merely Adornment—They Influence Our Lives

In our modern world today we give our children fancy names without looking at the meanings of the names. I have been guilty of this. If I knew then what I know today concerning the impact and influence of a name, I would have chosen names for my children differently, but I thank God we have prayed over our children's names and broken every negative spirit. As a child of God, I find it important to understand we should not select names simply because we like the sound of them. It is crucial to understand the spirit behind any name we choose. Our name influences our character, actions, and attitudes in ways we cannot fully comprehend. Proverbs 22:1 says, "A good name is more desirable [to be chosen] than great riches; to be esteemed is better than silver or gold." Proverbs here uses the words "better than" to emphasize the value, importance, and magnitude of a good name. Riches certainly are great thing to have and are a gift from God if acquired honestly. However, wealth is not nearly as important as a good name or reputation. It is better to have a reputable name than to have great wealth, because a name speaks volumes about a person's inner character. Furthermore, it essentially displays the heart of God in such a person. Our personal name, as well as our name or reputation in society, is crucial to the advancement of the kingdom of God.

As Christians we must realize that having a good standing in society is important as we share the good news of the kingdom of God. If people consider us bad simply because we are preaching the good news of the kingdom of God, we should give it no thought. However, if they consider us bad because of our character, attitude, or actions, then we need to ask ourselves this: Do my character or actions really reflect the character of God and His Son, Jesus Christ? Just as our personal name influences our life, so our reputation in the community as Christians influences others. We can either attract people to God or discourage them from following Him.

Likewise, a church's reputation can either attract people or discourage them from attending. A church with a great reputation for teaching sound doctrine should be desirable to all kingdom-minded people above one that teaches a diluted gospel that appeals to the itching ears of people. Just as people go after name brands when it comes to quality products, we must go after sound doctrine as our main brand name and never trade that for a lower quality, cheaper, shallow, and man-pleasing gospel. If you are a pastor, evangelist, apostle, or minister, let people know you for your quality and uncompromised gospel of Jesus Christ and for standing on the name of Jesus Christ.

In Christ we have a good name and reputation, not because of our spirituality or religiosity but because we stand on the name that is above all names—the name of Jesus Christ. In Christ and with Christ, we have a good name in society, and a good name is better than any amount of gold or silver. A good name is trusted because it provides stability and comfort. The name of Jesus Christ is better than any other name for it is trustworthy, stable, and unchangeable. Standing on the name of Jesus Christ is standing on solid, unshakable, immovable ground. Jesus' name is reliable. When we call on His name, demons flee, sickness goes, and the weak and fearful become stronger. The name of Jesus Christ must truly be an influential part of our lives and the very foundation of our faith and stability in God. In His name, we have the power of God and live, move, breathe, and have our being. Without the power of the name of Jesus Christ, we are powerless and lifeless.

## A Name May Remind You of the Past—Good or Bad

Names not only influence but also trigger memories—both good and bad. For example, in 1 Samuel 7:12 after the men of Israel had defeated the Philistines at Mizpah, Samuel took a stone and set it up between

Mizpah and Shen and named it Ebenezer, meaning "thus far the Lord has helped us." Samuel wanted to remind himself, his generation, and generations to come how the Lord had helped them defeat the Philistines at Mizpah. Likewise, your name may be a memorial of something good in your parent's past so it would forever trigger that good memory.

The mention of *Jabez* in 1 Chronicles 4:9–10 is a good example. His mother named him Jabez, saying, "Because I bore him with pain." The name Jabez is a close variant of the Hebrew word for *pain*. Pain is simply suffering, torment, or discomfort. This means his mother associated Jabez's name with the suffering she had experienced in childbirth. Though the details of that pain are not disclosed to us in the text, we do know the name Jabez reminded his mother of it. However, the name was obviously going to be a hindrance to the future of Jabez, so he cried out to the God of Israel, saying, "Oh that you would bless me indeed and enlarge my border, and that your hand might be with me, and that you would keep me from harm that it may not pain me" (1 Chronicles 4:10 NASB). This profound prayer and cry to the Lord changed the course of Jabez's life, for the Lord heard his prayer and granted his request.

First Chronicles 4:10 confirms the significance of a name: "Please pay no attention, my Lord, to that wicked man Nabal. He is just like his name—his name means fool, and folly goes with him." The name Nabal means "fool," and in the text we see that Nabal acted foolish. Indeed, his name called out for the spirit of foolishness to influence his life. Negative names affect people, producing a deficiency in character. Whatever meaning or influence your name carries, if you cry out to the Lord Jesus Christ, He has the power to turn a bad influence into a good one. He can pour out His life on your name and sanctify it and destroy its bad influence on your life, family, and future so you can live your life just as God created you to live. Allow the Holy Spirit to breathe new life into your name and break the limitations it imposes so you can thrive in Christ.

A final example of how a name can act as a reminder can be found in the first chapter of the book of Hosea. God instructed Hosea to give specific names to his three children from his unfaithful, promiscuous wife, Gomer—names that would remind His people of their unfaithfulness toward Him. Each name had a meaning that revealed the action God was going to take against the people.

The first name, given to his first son, was Jezreel, which meant "God will scatter." The second name, given to his daughter, was Lo–ruhammah, which meant "no compassion," and the third and final name, given to his second son, was Lo–ammi, which meant "not my people." All these names signified what the people had become in the eyes of God because of their unfaithfulness, and each name demonstrated the action God was about to take. God was going to scatter them. He was going to show them no compassion because their actions demonstrated they were not His people. Of course, we see God showing mercy on them later. Just as Hosea, whose name means "salvation," redeemed his unfaithful wife, so God would bring salvation to them, redeem them, gather them again, and call them His own people (Hosea 3:1). A name, good or bad, carries something significant. It may represent good memories or bad memories. Mentioning the name of Jesus Christ brings great and precious memories of the redemptive work and salvation of God for all humankind. The name of Jesus Christ is a symbol or sign of God's power, mercy, grace, life, redemption, rest, hope, and salvation, which come only through Jesus.

## Moses Questioned God: What Is Your Name?

The ancient world—much like the modern one—had many false gods that claimed various powers, and they all had names that in some way revealed their character. For example, Baal was a title meaning "lord." He was a supreme false god worshipped in ancient

Canaan and Phoenicia as a fertility god, believed to enable the earth to produce crops and people to produce children. In other words, Baal gave false promises of fertility to people, for God is the only true living God who has power to give life.

When God appeared to Moses and called him to rescue the children of Israel (Exodus 3:13–14), Moses asked God what His name was. Why? Moses wanted to know the name of Yahweh because His name could give him and the children of Israel an idea of His power and ability to deliver them from the power of Pharaoh and his gods. Moses wanted to know what made Yahweh different from those false and powerless gods like Baal that many people in the ancient world worshipped and looked to for assistance. Psalm 135:15–18 describes these false gods:

> They are gods made by human hands, they have mouths, but do not speak, they have eyes, but do not see; they have ears, but do not hear and above all, they don't have any breath in them, they are lifeless and powerless.

**What Does the Name of God Reveal to Us?**

To know God's names is to know His nature, character, and attributes. To know His names is to know the origin of His power, who He really is, what He does, and what He can do. When you know the power behind the names of God, you will grasp who God really is to you as His child, and you will discover who He wants to be in your life today. In Exodus 3:14 God introduced Himself to Moses as "I AM WHO I AM" (in Hebrew *ehyeh asher ehyeh*). "I am who I am" first describes God as uncreated (Genesis 1:1). He is self-existent and unchanging. He Himself is the beginning and the end; beside Him there is no other true God. He is the creator and sustainer of all that exists, and He is the same yesterday and today and forever (Hebrews 13:8). "I am who I am" also reveals God's strength and power to do extraordinary things, which no false god of Pharaoh could do. The name signified to Moses God's strength, authority, and power to deliver the children of Israel from the powerful hands of Pharaoh.

In the Bible the names of God and the being of God are closely related—His names denote power, authority, and dominion over any other gods. His actions of creation, love, mercy, forgiveness, judgment, and punishment are related to His character and nature. Discovering the power in the name of God is crucial because it helps us discover the power we have in God and through Him. It was important for Moses to know the name of the God who was sending him out to rescue the people because so many false gods were worshipped at that time. Even today we face the challenge of false gods and false prophets masquerading as being from God. They perform miracles in the name of God, but they are not from God, do not have His Spirit, and have no true power from the kingdom of God. If we are not sensitive to leading of the Holy Spirit, we may not correctly discern these imposters.

One of the easiest ways to recognize false gods and their representatives is by examining the doctrinal teachings and spiritual fruits that flow from them. The ambassadors of false gods have no sound doctrines and do not reflect the character of the true God. God is still healing the sick, setting the captives free, and performing signs and wonders through ordinary people who have given themselves over to the leading of the Holy Spirit in their lives and bring glory and honor to the name of God. But some people with wrong motives have misused the name of God for their personal gain. This is why the Bible says, "Dear brothers, do not believe every spirit, but test the spirits to see whether they are from God, because many false prophets have gone out into the world" (1 John 4:1).

## The Enemy Likes Hiding behind the Name of Jesus

Satan likes hiding behind the name of Jesus and using it because it is the most influential and powerful name there is. He knows people pay attention when they hear our Savior's name. Yet interestingly, even the demons can recognize if a person is from God or is just hiding behind the name of God.

Acts 19:11–16 describes some people who tried to use the name of Jesus Christ in the same way Paul did to cast out demons, even though they themselves were practicing sorcery. We are told, "God did extraordinary miracles through Paul, so that even handkerchiefs and aprons that had touched him were taken to the sick, and their illnesses were cured and the evil spirits left them." Some Jews who went around driving out evil spirits tried to invoke the name of the Lord Jesus over those who were demon-possessed, saying, "In the name of the Jesus whom Paul preaches, I command you to come out." Among the culprits hiding behind the name of Jesus were the seven sons of Sceva, a Jewish chief priest. But one day an evil spirit answered them as they tried to cast it out of a person, saying, "Jesus I know, and Paul I know about, but who are you?" Then the man who had the evil spirit jumped on them, overpowered them all, and gave them such a ferocious beating that they ran out of the house naked and bleeding.

The seven sons of Sceva had attempted to use Jesus' divine name to command evil spirits to come out, but they did not share in Christ's divine authority and power through faith in Him as Paul did. It takes more than the invocation of the powerful name of Jesus Christ to defeat the forces of darkness. To cast out evil spirits we must be in fellowship with Christ, and Christ's power must be in us through faith. We can't hide behind the name of Jesus Christ. Jesus' Spirit must be in us and we must be in Him to walk in His power and anointing. There are consequences to invoking the name of Jesus Christ against demonic forces when Jesus is not in us.

The name of Jesus Christ must be held in high honor and not misused for our own personal gain or for showing off. The power and anointing in the name of Jesus are not for showmanship. His name is not to be used to control or manipulate. His power is available to those who are concerned about what God is concerned about—setting the captives free to His glory and honor. If you are in Christ and are submitted to His leadership through His name, you have power to cast out demons and authority over any forces of darkness. When you are in Christ and He is in you, you can never be defeated by evil.

**You Have Authority through the Name of Jesus**

*The believer's power, authority, and dominion over any spiritual forces of this world rest in the power that is in the name of Jesus Christ. The Hebrew names of God recorded in the Bible illustrate the power we have in God and who God really is and how He relates to our life situations and struggles.*

*He Is Our Elohim*

The name Elohim, which occurs over 2,500 times in the Old Testament, reminds us that our God is the God of gods (Deuteronomy 10:17; Psalm 136:2), the only true God, and the creator of the heavens and the sea and all that is within them. He is the majestic ruler who has demonstrated His awesome power in many dimensions of life (Psalm 68) throughout the history of humankind; consequently, He will not and cannot let you down or fail you.

*Dr. Kazumba Charles*

*He Is Our El Shaddai*

The name El Shaddai is used in the longer form seven times in the Bible (Genesis 17:1; 28:3; 35:11; 43:14; 48:3; Exodus 6:3; Ezekiel 10:5) and more frequently in the shorter form Shaddai (thirty times in Job; Psalm 19:1; 68:14; Ruth 1:21; Isaiah 13:6; Ezekiel 1:24; Joel 1:15). In all these passages the name speaks of God as our all-powerful, all-sufficient, transcendent, and sovereign ruler. Never give up in life unless God says it's over, but if He hasn't said so, keep pushing forward in life, and He will stand by you and with you.

*He Is Our Yahweh*

The name Yahweh is a distinctly proper name of God. It is never used to refer to any pagan gods, and it never refers to men. It appears 5,321 times in the Old Testament, appearing first in Genesis 2:4, where it is joined with Elohim. Yahweh is used 164 times in Genesis, and it appears 1,800 times in Exodus through Joshua. According to most Bible scholars, the exact meaning of the name Yahweh is difficult to determine, but most agree it is related to the verb meaning "to be," "cause to be," "I am," or "I shall be." If this is the case, then Exodus 3:14 could be translated as follows: "I shall be what I say I shall be." God will be to us who He says He will be, no matter what. So if you are sick, He will be what He says He will be to you: *Yahweh–rapha,* your healer (Exodus 15:26). If you don't have a shepherd or someone to guide you, He will be your *Yahweh–rohi,* your shepherd (Ezekiel 34:15). If you are lacking anything, He will be to you *Yahweh–jireh,* your provider (Genesis 22:14). And if you don't have peace, He will be to you *Yahweh–shalom,* your peace. If you are going through a difficult situation, you don't need to panic or throw in the towel because of the stress that comes with the challenges. You just need to stand still in the unfailing name of God and let the shalom presence of God overwhelm your life and bring peace to your heart. Your battle belongs to God.

*He Is Our Adonai*

The name Adonai means "God is our master, ruler, and Lord. "We belong to Him alone, and if we humbly submit to Him and fear Him, we need to fear nothing in life. Adonai appears about 360 times in the Old Testament, though it is not used in the same way every time. It is first found in Genesis 15:2 and 15:8 when Abram requested more definite information concerning a son and the promised land. It appears only fourteen times after that in the Pentateuch. It appears over fifty times in the Psalms. Certain prophets like Isaiah, Jeremiah, Ezekiel, and Amos used it frequently also. The name Adonai expresses faith, assurance, security, and thanksgiving (Psalm 16:2; 57:9–10). God is our assurance and security.

*He Is Our Alpha and Omega*

God is our Alpha and Omega—that is, our beginning and end. *Alpha* and *omega* are the first and last letters of the Greek alphabet. God declares in the book of Revelation that He, as well as His Son, is the Alpha and Omega (1:8; 21:6, 22:13). These words emphasize His continuous existence—from A to Z. From the beginning to the end of all creation, God is God, and He will continue to be God and all He says He is to us. Everything in our life must begin and end with God and must bring glory and honor to His holy name.

Just as all the names of God the Father remind us of who God is to us, all Jesus' names recorded in the Bible remind us of who we are in Christ and what we have in Him. Jesus is our Immanuel—God with us (Isaiah 7:14). He is our Yeshua—the one who saves us (Matthew 1:21). He is our Prince of Peace—the one who gives peace (Isaiah

9:6). He is our Christ—the Anointed One (Matthew 16:16). He is our King of kings—the ruler of all people (Revelation 19:16). He is the author of life—the one who gives us life (Acts 3:15). He is our mighty God—the defender of our lives (Isaiah 9:6). He is our Wonderful Counselor (Isaiah 9:6)—He gives us wise counsel through the Holy Spirit. He is our advocate—the one who intercedes or pleads our case to God the Father (1 John 2:1). And He is the beginning and the end, who is and is to come (Revelation 1:8).

If we grasp the function and power behind the names of God, we can surely discover the power we have in Him. When we look at some of the names of God through the mind-set of the ancient Hebrews, we find that the names have power, fame, honor, renown, and a good report behind them. Each name displays His majestic power and character to the world. The ancient Hebrews understood God in a concrete fashion as a tangible God who can be heard even though He can't be seen—not as a God who is far removed from us.

Philippians 2:10 shows us the power behind the name of Jesus Christ: "At the name of Jesus every knee will bow, of those who are in heaven and on earth and under the earth and every tongue should confess that Jesus Christ is Lord, to the glory of God the Father." Romans 10:13 declares, "For everyone who calls on the name of the Lord will be saved." When we understand who God is and the fame and power of His name, we will be more than willing to declare His name to all the nations from generation to generation (Psalm 22:22). His names clearly teach that He is the all-powerful God who alone is self-existent and self-sufficient. Only God has life in and of Himself. No one is like Him or can come close to being like Him. He is majestic in His name and in His works.

## His Name Is Your Weapon of Spiritual Warfare

You cannot function in the power of your gifts without the power of God. Through the name of Jesus Christ, God has given you all the power you need in life to do His will and be all that He has called you to be. Jesus' name is your source of joy and strength. It delivers you from sickness and enables you to do great things for the kingdom of God. His name is your shield and protection, and only in His name can you break the chains that stop you from moving forward in life. Whatever you do, stand on the name of Jesus Christ, and let it be the hallmark of your life, marriage, future, and destiny. Your gifts are only as good and powerful as the power behind them. If Jesus Christ is not the power behind your gifts, You will find it difficult to do anything for the kingdom of God. As you pray, pray in the name of Jesus Christ. When you pray in His name, you pray with His authority and dominion, and God will answer your prayers.

To move forward successfully and be all God created you to be, you need to discover the power you have through the name of Jesus Christ. The name of Jesus Christ is your weapon of spiritual warfare; your strong tower (Proverbs 18:10); your rock, refuge, and salvation (2 Samuel 22:3); your fortress, deliverer, and shield (Psalm 18:2). Above all, the name of Jesus Christ is a tower of your strength against all your enemies (Psalm 61:3).

The greatest mistake people can make is to put their trust in the "name" of money, career, people, or anything else of this world. All such things are powerless and can come and go, but the name of Jesus can never let you down or disappoint you. Man can disappoint you, but not Jesus Christ. When you put your faith and trust in Him and His abilities, you are standing on a solid rock of ages that has never failed and will never fail. Whatever you desire to be in life, surrender your desire to the power of the name of Jesus Christ. Pray in His name (John 14:13), and through His name you will do great things for the kingdom of God.

It is important to understand that the name of Jesus is not a magical name or a vending machine. It's a name that works powerfully by first developing your relationship and intimacy with Jesus Christ, the Holy Spirit, and God the Father.

In our next chapter we will look at how you can fully function in the gifts God has graced you with and bring glory and honor to Him and advance His kingdom in the hearts of many people.

## Chapter 5

# FUNCTIONING IN THE POWER OF YOUR GIFTS

God Has Given You Tools to Succeed in Life

Every believer in Christ in today's world must consciously ask these questions:

Why has God gifted me?
Why has God given me His Holy Spirit?
Why would God choose to share His power, authority, and dominion with me?
Why am I a Christian?
Why am I saved by the blood of Jesus Christ and called by God?
Why does God want to anoint and empower me?
The Bible says we are a chosen generation, a royal priesthood, a holy nation, and God's special possession (1 Peter 2:9). What does that mean and how should I respond?
Am I called just to attend church, be a good Christian, and sit around doing nothing until I go to heaven?

We must ask and answer these crucial questions if we are to step out of our comfort zone and function in the power and anointing of the gifts God has graciously given us to glorify and honor His name and advance His purpose, plan, and will.

Too many men and women of God today are living in a spiritual dilemma. They feel unfulfilled and have no purpose or direction in life simply because they have not yet discovered how they can put their gifts to work so they can function in life as God designed them to do. Many Christians also have given up on their gifts and callings because people have discouraged them or because they have convinced themselves they are not good enough. But in God we don't have to be good enough and we don't have to feel as if we don't qualify. Why? Because it is through the goodness and grace of Jesus Christ that we are children of God who have placed our faith in the name of Jesus Christ and been qualified to be ambassadors of the kingdom of God.

God is not looking or waiting for you to be perfect before He can use you mightily. He already knows you are not perfect; all He requires from you is your obedience and humility to do what He asks of you. Everything else in your life will slowly be taken care of as your respond to the Word of God in the power of the Holy Spirit and as you continue to surrender your life and all that concerns you to the power of God.

One of the most sobering truths in life is that until you do what God gifted and anointed you to do, you will never be a happy person. You can try, but you will always feel empty and broken. This is why many people with high-paying jobs and great careers are never satisfied and always feel as if something is missing. They are right. Something is missing—the will, plan, and purpose of God in their lives. When people find God's will for their lives, they thrive and excel at everything their hands touch because God's will always prevails (Proverbs 19:21); it cannot be thwarted (Isaiah 14:27).

When you personally discover the plan of God for your life, nothing can stop you from functioning in the power of the gifts of God within you or from excelling in life. If you are not using your gifts, is it because you are waiting for someone to discover you or because you have been told you are not good enough? Or do you even know you have gifts from God that will benefit the body of Christ?

The goal of this chapter is to ignite your gifts and passion for God so you can function in the body of Christ as you were created to do. To discover and understand how we can all function in the power of our gifts as well as work within our ministry offices to change the world, we are going to examine 1 Corinthians 12:4–31 and Ephesians 4:11–16.

As a Christian you need to understand that if you don't know your gift or your ministry office or God's purpose and plan for your life, you will find it extremely difficult to step out and do exploits for the kingdom of God. Moreover, if you are not operating in your gifts or calling, you will end up unfulfilled, unhappy, disgruntled, and disappointed. You may move from one church to another trying to find a church that fits you while what you are really searching for is a place where you can groom your skills, talents, and gifts and put them to proper use in the local church and in ministry outside the local church.

As a former soccer player, I know the importance of the coach positioning his or her players according to their abilities so each player is in the best place for the team to play effectively and overcome their opponents. A great coach will not put a goalie in an offensive position, especially if he or she has skilled offensive players on his or her team. Neither will the coach put a good offensive player in a defensive position. Doing this would make the team weak. But when a coach puts all his or her players in their best positions according to their abilities and everyone is doing what he or she has been trained to do, the team stands a much better chance of winning the game. Teamwork and proper use of players lead to a winning team.

God is a great "coach," and He has a winning formula for the church against the enemy. He has given the body of Christ a diversity of spiritual gifts to use against the powers of the kingdom of darkness so that through the church He can set people free from Satan's influence on their lives. If these gifts are not put into their proper positions, the enemy will continue to influence many people. The kingdom of God is all about teamwork; it is not a one-man show. For the kingdom of God to forcefully advance in our communities and set the captives free, apostles must be in their spiritual position doing the work of apostles (not just walking boastfully in that title while doing nothing). Prophets must be in their spiritual positions prophesying what they hear from God (not what they hear from their minds or what people want to hear from them). Evangelists must be in their spiritual positions as the feet and legs of the church, going into the communities and nations proclaiming the good news of the kingdom of God (not just counting how many nations or places they have preached or visited). Pastors must be in their spiritual positions being great shepherds and leading God's people with Christ-like compassion (not using the Word of God to beat down people but to uplift and set them free from the power of sin and death). And teachers must be in their spiritual positions teaching the undiluted, sound doctrines of God (not teaching a diluted gospel that comforts people in their sin).

The church today is ineffective and somewhat dysfunctional simply because most spiritual gifts are operating out of their positions or have been cut off completely by their insecurities. The evangelist wants to be an apostle (because the title sounds much more impressive), the pastor wants to be a prophet (because prophecy attracts many people and today it's the money-maker), and the teacher wants to be an evangelist in order to gather many people to himself or herself.

With such confusion, the body of Christ cannot win the lost from the demonic forces of this world. It takes the unity of gifts working together to destroy the kingdom of darkness.

It is easy to identify the reason we are not powerfully functioning in the gifts God has bestowed on each of us: disunity and competitiveness among men and women of God who desire to be great and are insecure when they see others operating in the same gifts or in the same ministry. This must change if we are to see God move in great ways. We need to embrace other gifts and never feel intimidated by them. We all belong to the same winning team—team Jesus. When one wins, we win together, and when one loses, we all lose.

The body of Christ needs to deal with today's challenge to bring all the spiritual gifts together, functioning in unity and according to God's design and purpose. God did not give spiritual gifts to the church for individuals to use in isolation; rather, the gifts are to work in cooperation with one another so the church can be an overcoming army of God and a place of healing, restoration, and revival. The spirit of insecurity or self-importance stops most of us from using our gifts to bless others. People tend to shut off other gifts or disregard them as unimportant because they are intimidated by what others could become in the kingdom of God. Many do not want to help others excel in their callings and gifts because they are afraid of being surpassed in one way or the other. That is an attitude of the devil. It cannot be of God because in the kingdom of God there is no competition—only encouragement and appreciation for each person's contribution to the work of God. If you feel insecure and intimidated by the gifts of others, ask yourself this question: Am I in this for my selfish gain or for the kingdom and glory of God?

Every spiritual gift God gave to the church is crucial and extremely important to the advancement of His kingdom and to the church's effectiveness and impact on a broken and divided society. We cannot disregard any spiritual gift and expect to impact the world for God. We need every gift God has blessed us with to do His work.

As you read this book, I want you to understand that you are a crucial part of the body of Christ. If someone has told you that you are useless or unimportant and that has kept you from doing anything for God, it's time for you to rise up and overcome that notion. Put your gifts to work to the glory and honor of the God who has graciously gifted you! You are a Christian, anointed by God, gifted by God, chosen by Him alone, and called a royal priesthood, a holy nation, and God's special possession. As such, you are called to arise and declare the praises of your God, who has rescued you out of the kingdom of darkness and brought you into His marvelous kingdom of light. You are to do what God has called you to do, not for people, not to be seen by people, and not to be praised by people, but in response to the graciousness and goodness of God in your life. Remember that He has shared His power and dominion with you. Walk and work in unity as a response to the mercy and goodness of God, who has called you to represent Him.

## Understanding the Importance of Unity and the Purpose of Spiritual Gifts

In 1 Corinthians 12:4 Paul writes about the importance and the unity of spiritual gifts:

> Now there are different gifts, but the same Spirit. And there are different ministries, but the same Lord. And there are different activities, but the same God activates each gift in each person. A demonstration of the Spirit is given to each person to produce what is beneficial: to one is given a

message of wisdom through the Spirit, to another, a message of knowledge by the same Spirit, to another, faith by the same Spirit, to another, gifts of healing by the one Spirit, to another, the performing of miracles, to another, prophecy, to another, distinguishing between spirits, to another, different kinds of languages, to another, interpretation of languages. But one and the same Spirit is active in all these, distributing to each person as He wills. (1 Corinthians 12:4–11)

One of the keys to functioning in the power of the gifts God has given to every one of us is understanding the importance of unity in the body of Christ and the purpose of the spiritual gifts. If we don't understand kingdom unity and the purpose of the gifts, we will live a life of selfishness and self-importance, and we will fear joining hands with other ministries to do the work of God. In 1 Corinthians 12 we see the great diversity of spiritual gifts, but what is interesting is that the same Spirit of God gives them all. The one triune God gives a variety of gifts to be used within the corporate body in a variety of ministries. These gifts work effectively in unity within the body of Christ and in unity with the Godhead (God the Father, Jesus, and the Holy Spirit).

We must each understand what our gifts are and realize they will differ from the gifts of many others. Never measure the importance of your gift against the gifts of other people. God created you in a unique way and put a unique gift or combination of gifts in you so you can function in His kingdom as you and not as someone else. When you discover your gifts and function in them without insecurity, you become unstoppable, happy, fulfilled, and passionately focused on what God has called you to do. Each of us needs to discover or rediscover his or her gifts and ministry calling in life. Only then can the church function as it should, changing lives and transforming communities all over the world.

God gives every spiritual gift to produce what is beneficial to the entire body of Christ. These gifts are not in competition with one another but complement each other when they are used in unity. Unfortunately, many of us have not fully grasped this concept. Consequently, some churches have split simply because one leader is gifted in a prophetic ministry while another is gifted with a healing gift. The one with a prophetic gift for some reason thinks he is superior, and the one with a healing gift thinks his gift is superior. The result is a split with one leaving and the church focusing on only one ministry. In fact, if we look closely at some local churches, we will find that quite often only one gift is dominant and functional—the rest of the gifts are absent or dormant. How can we expect to do exploits for the kingdom of God with only one gift operational? God gave the local church many gifts to use to advance His kingdom and build up one another in faith.

Until we collectively understand the unity of spiritual gifts, we will never walk in the fullness of the revival fire of God. Your gift brings a certain fire of God to the church, and another person's gift brings in a different type fire, and my gift brings in yet another fire. When we combine these gifts, we can have a true and sustainable fire of God breaking out in the church as well as in the nations.

**One Body with Many Parts—Diversity**

> For as the body is one and has many parts, and all the parts of that body, though many, are one body—so also is Christ. For we were all baptized by one Spirit in to one body—whether Jews or Greeks, whether slaves or free—and we were all made to

drink of one Spirit. So the body is not one part but many—If the foot should say, "Because I'm not a hand, I don't belong to the body," in spite of this it still belongs to the body—And if the ear should say, "Because I'm not an eye, I don't belong to the body," in spite of this it still belongs to the body. If the whole body were an eye, where would the hearing be? If the whole body were an ear, where would the sense of smell be? But now God has placed each one of the parts in one body just as He wanted. And if they were all the same part, where would the body be? Now they are many parts, yet one body. So the eye cannot say to the hand, "I don't need you!" Or again, the head can't say to the feet, "I don't need you!" But even more, those parts of the body that seem to be weaker are necessary. And those parts of the body that we think to be less honorable, we clothe these with greater honor, and our unpresentable parts have a better presentation. (1 Corinthians 12:12–22)

The apostle Paul here was teaching the church at Corinth and the body of Christ at large about the importance of diversity in the kingdom of God. He was also teaching the believers in Corinth the impact of unity and the proper functioning of spiritual gifts—as well as giving instruction on Christian living. Paul had received some disturbing information concerning the spiritual condition of the church at Corinth. It was reported to him that there were factions (see 1 Corinthians 1:11) and moral problems (see chapters 5–6) in the Corinthian church. While the church was extremely gifted (see 1 Corinthians 1:4–7), it was also immature and unspiritual (3:1–4). Consequently, they couldn't use the gifts of God properly.

Where there is immaturity there is instability, division, jealousy, hatred, envy, and pride—but above all there is a misuse of both spiritual gifts and authority. In such an environment some people think of themselves as more special than others. Paul thus gave the example of the functioning of a human body as a model for how the body of Christ should function. Just as a foot cannot say, "Because I am not the hand, I don't belong to the body," a person with a gift of healing cannot say, "Because I am not the lead pastor or I am not a prophet, I don't belong to the church." What does this mean for you and me? It means that just because we are not graced with one gift does not mean we should give up and do nothing for the kingdom of God. If we look carefully into our souls, we will each find we have a unique and important gift and should not feel worthless.

The church is one body, and yet it has many different parts. Every part within the body has an important task to perform. Even parts we are tempted to think are less important, fragile, or weaker are crucial to a complete, healthy, and functioning body. God intentionally gifted each one of us differently so we could function properly as His one body. We can't say to a person gifted in prophecy, "We don't need you here because we are a healing-gifted church." We need to find a balance in the body of Christ and equip and encourage men and women of God to function in the area of their gifts if we are to forcefully and peacefully advance God's kingdom here on earth. The head (leader) needs all the parts of the body, for a head without legs, hands, feet, eyes, ears, or mouth is useless and dysfunctional. When the church clearly grasps this revelation, we will treat one another with dignity and honor, embrace each person's gift, and work in unity as one army of the Lord.

Jesus is the head of His church, and because He is the head, He requires His people (parts) to function in unity and in the power of their gifts with the Word of God to release His rule and reign in the nations. This means we must be willing to let other parts of the body operate in the body of Christ without manipulation or restriction but with true spiritual guidance. Each part of the body functions at its best when it is allowed, trained, and trusted to perform its designed duties freely. Training, trust, and encouragement are crucial to reviving a dysfunctional church and getting every part of the body to work effectively for one goal, purpose, and desire—the kingdom of God.

People's gifts are cultivated by giving them an opportunity to use them. Yes, this comes at a cost. Mistakes will be made, but with a great and visionary leader (coach) in place, those mistakes will soon be turned into a training ground for growth and maturity. Nobody can grow spiritually without making mistakes or experiencing setbacks or failures. The greatest thing about the kingdom of God is that in God's kingdom there is no losing; there are only winning and learning and gaining experiences from our failures. When things don't go your way, don't live in regret. Just ask yourself what you have learned from your experience.

## The Dynamic Power of Diversity

> He personally gave some to be apostles, some prophets, some evangelists, some pastors and teachers, for the training of the saints in the work of ministry, to build up the body of Christ, until we all reach unity in the faith and in the knowledge of God's son, growing into a mature man with a stature measured by Christ's fullness. Then we will no longer be little children, tossed by the waves and blown around by every wind of teaching, by human cunning with cleverness in the techniques of deceit. (Ephesians 4:11–16)

If you envy other people and aspire to be someone other than who God created you to be, you will find it difficult to step into the destiny God set for you before the beginning of time. Countless people fail to unleash the dynamic power within them because they are afraid to embrace their calling. I know people who have many titles and yet are frustrated because they are trying to find themselves in a title instead of the ministry the title represents. Your ministry position or title is not who you are; it simply represents what you do or should be doing for the kingdom of God. Imagine for a second a church where apostles are effectively functioning as true apostles, prophets are hearing from God and prophesying the true word from God, evangelists are bringing lost souls into the kingdom of God, pastors are shepherding God's flock with the Spirit and heart of God, and teachers are teaching nothing but the pure Word of God and equipping God's people to do the work of ministry. How powerful could such a church be?

The church can be extremely influential in the communities of the nations. We as Christians can move in the dynamic power of God if the various gifts are embraced and allowed to work in unity and in submission to one another and the spiritual leadership of the church. When Paul says God gave some to be apostles, some prophets, some evangelists, some pastors and teachers, he is not talking about titles or individualism or the prestige of having a title. Rather, he is talking about the functioning of an apostle, prophet, evangelist, pastor, and teacher within a united body of Christ. Many people run after titles, but they fail to function in the power of that title because their focus is on a position or title rather than on the purpose or task associated with the title or position. God has given to the body of Christ gifts to accomplish His mission of reaching His people through His Word, love, and grace. Gifts are for serving one another in love and humility (see Galatians 5:13; Philippians 2:3). Every true gift from the Spirit of God comes to uplift, heal, restore, empower, and build up God's people, not to destroy them or destabilize the church.

## Spiritual Gifts Are for Divine Mission

In the early church an apostle had a divine mission or task to accomplish. So did the prophet, evangelist, pastor, and teacher of the Word. An apostle sometimes served as spokesman for God by bringing a new revelation and understanding to the church. Prophets also had a responsibility to reveal God's will to believers both for the present (forth-telling) and the future (fore-telling). Evangelists had a clear objective too. They were gifted to spread the gospel and plant churches. Furthermore, they proclaimed the good news in word and deed and instructed others in evangelism. The pastor's duty was to provide oversight, comfort, and guidance to the local church and to shepherd God's people through the Word of God (see Acts 20:28; 1 Peter 5:1–4). The teacher's role was to instruct and help God's people apply the Word of God to their lives. Teachers of the Word of God were concerned with passing on the church's revealed sound teachings (see 1 Corinthians 15:3–4) and helping people avoid falling into false doctrines. When a church has an apostle, a prophet, an evangelist, a pastor, and a teacher diligently carrying out their responsibilities in unity, humility, and love for God's people, the result is a kingdom explosion and true revival and reformation.

The purposes of the gifts you possess or the ministry office you occupy are to build the body of Christ and equip others to do the work of ministry. Thus, whatever you do, do it to the glory and honor of God and serve others. Your gift or ministry office is just as important and needed as any other. This is why I challenge you to function in your gifts, whatever they may be. Too many people are yet to discover and activate their gifts. One goal of this book is to help you discover and activate your gifts and use them to bless others.

This is your time to rise up and be what God created you to be and do what He anointed you to do for His kingdom even before you were born. You were created for a purpose, and you have been endowed with the power (*dunamis*) of God so you can be a witness of the goodness of God's kingdom (Acts 1:8).

Our master, Jesus Christ, wants us all to function in the body of Christ. The more we do what He has called us to do, the more our faith increases so we grow spiritually and become mature Christians. Living for God requires us to exercise our faith by being doers of God's Word. In other words, we are to practice the Word of God and put our faith to work every day. Just as an athlete practices before the actual game, we believers in Christ practice love and exercise our faith in church before stepping out into the world and demonstrating God's love and power.

If you don't put your gift to work or exercise your ministry gift in real life, your faith, passion, desire for God, and zeal for the things of God will be quenched and slowly disappear. Many people who backslide or give up on following Jesus Christ are those who do not actively live out or exercise their faith by serving God with their gifts. When you are actively involved in the work of ministry, your mind becomes more focused on the kingdom of God and less focused on the ungodly things of this world. You are set free to do the work of God and proclaim the praises of our God. When you truly know God and know His ways and desires, you will not sit around and do nothing; you will respond with everything within you to serve Him and allow Him to use you to set others free from anything that hinders them from living transformed lives.

**Set Free to Function as Kings and Priests**

Through the blood of Jesus Christ, God has set us free from the power of sin and death and rescued us from the influences of the kingdom of darkness so we can now live our life not for ourselves but for God. Furthermore, as God's children we can illustrate to the world His characteristics and nature and make His name known to the ends of the earth. We are set free to be ambassadors of God, bringing His kingdom into the hearts of the brokenhearted and the sick and bringing the life of Christ to lost souls. When we understand that the blood of Jesus Christ redeemed us for a purpose, our lives will be divinely motivated and directed.

Many Christians live with no purpose, no direction, and no passion simply because they have not yet discovered why God set them free and honored them by appointing them kings and priests to serve in His kingdom. Revelation 1:5–6 helps us understand the reason: "To Him who loved us and washed us from our sins in His own blood, and has made us kings and priests to His God and Father, to Him be glory and dominion forever and ever. Amen" (NKJV). In 1 Peter 2:9 Peter tells us, "You are a chosen race, a royal priesthood, a holy nation, a people for His possession, so that you may proclaim the praises of the One who called you out of darkness into His marvellous light."

As we read these two passages, it is important to ask two questions: Why has God made us a kingdom and priests? And are we just a kingdom of kings and priests without any duties? To uncover our kingdom call, we need first to look at the divine role of kings and priests in the ancient world. Kings and priests in the Middle Eastern culture played a significant role between God and the people God had entrusted to them. They were like advocates or messengers of God. One of the king's duties was to lead people to God and follow His ordinances, while the priests were to offer sacrifices to God on behalf of people. So these kings and priests were not just to sit in their anointed seats doing nothing all day. They had important tasks to perform.

The Hebrew word for *king* is the noun *melekh*. The corresponding verb simply means "to reign" or "to be king" and in turn is derived from a word that means "to possess." Kings were anointed by God to be the moral representative of the people for covenant purposes. The behavior of the king therefore was important to God's covenant with His people. Many kings failed to represent God until He sent the King of kings, who fulfilled all the functions of a king and priest and became the King forever. But He did not stop there. He made us kings and priests too so we can function in a kingly anointing, representing people before God and living our lives as covenant people of God. When a king is reigning, we call his realm a kingdom; consequently, we are kings in God's kingdom only when we rule and reign through Him or function according to the King's (Jesus Christ's) anointing and display the characteristics of His kingdom to the world.

When we look at the meaning of the word *king,* we can see that when John declares that God "has made us kings and priests," he is not focusing on a greater or higher title that is above other titles. Rather, he is talking about the function of kings and priests. There is no king without authority or a kingdom. A king is called a king because he has a kingdom over which he reigns. God has made us kings so that through us He can reign over and posses the nations with the good news of His kingdom. We are to be kings, meaning we are to function in the power and authority of Christ our King, who is the King of kings.

When you declare you are a "King's kid," remember this: your life, attitude, and character must reflect Jesus Christ, the King of kings. As king He reigns with love, mercy, authority, power, and grace. Furthermore, He reigns with justice, forgiveness, and a heart full of compassion. In Him there is no injustice, prejudice, unforgiveness, or hatred. He is indeed a true reflection of the kingdom of heaven.

## As a Christian You Have a Kingdom Mission

Revelation 1:5–6 indicates that all believers who have been grafted into the biblical heritage of Israel are a kingdom (kings) and priests. The titles and mission already designated for Israel (see Exodus 19:6) have been extended to all believers, whether Jew or Gentile. We are kings and priests so we can serve God and reign on earth with Him (see Revelation 5:10; 20:6). As priests of God, we see that our duty is to offer the incense of prayer to God on behalf of the people and nations (Revelation 5:8). As kings, we know must reign in the power, authority, and anointing of God. God wants to work through us to release the authority of His kingdom and all the its benefits upon the earth. This cannot be achieved through a few leaders but only through the entire body of Christ, which means we are all important parts of the body and needed for such a time as this.

Peter says we are a chosen race, a royal priesthood, a holy nation, and a people of God's possession. And John says Jesus has made us kings, or a kingdom and priests. Again, it is important to understand that their focus is not on the titles but on the responsibilities that come with the titles. This doesn't mean that a title is bad and that we shouldn't seek one, but it does mean that before we jump into any spiritual office or accept a title, we must clearly understand the responsibilities so we can function in it with the heart of God and not with arrogance or pride. God is not concerned about titles—He is concerned about how we function in the office where He has placed us. It is the natural man who is so concerned about the prestige of a title. This is why some people have great titles but are dysfunctional. Remember that we are a royal priesthood, kings, priests, and a race chosen for a purpose. Jesus Christ has set us free from the power of sin and death so we can carry out our mission and *function* as kings and priests. Moreover, we are called to priesthood so we can administer God's love to others and demonstrate to the world the nature of who He is. As priests and kings anointed by

God, we are responsible for demonstrating the character of God to the nations and facilitating the work of God.

## A Higher Calling Comes with Greater Responsibilities

The kingship and priesthood to which God has called us come with serious moral imperatives and responsibilities. Many kings and priests in the Old Testament era failed God because they slipped into moral degradation or did not take their responsibilities seriously; hence, they could not purely represent God in their communities or shepherd His people with His compassionate heart. They abused their offices by mistreating or taking advantage of the people God had called them to serve and lead on His behalf. As kings and priests unto our God, we need to understand the responsibilities we have because in the kingdom of God the higher our calling, the greater the responsibilities are. Luke 12:48 puts it into perspective for us: "To whom much is given, from him much is expected."

Much is required of you as a Christian, as a king, and as a priest. Throughout the Hebrew Bible, the term *priest* (*kōhēn*) is commonly used to refer to an official who was set apart from the rest of the community to carry out certain duties associated with worship and sacrifice. You have been set apart from a worldly community or culture to a kingdom community and culture. This means your life must reflect the new you and not carry on as the old you—something must change. Yes! You cannot be perfect, of course, and God does not expect you to be, but your spirit must be different from the spirit of the world.

As a minister of the Lord (Joel 1:9; 2:17), a priest functioned as a mediator of God's presence and was responsible for the day-to-day operation of the sacrificial system. As priests we are set apart to offer an acceptable sacrifice and worship to our God on behalf of the nations. God has made us kings and priests, not for decorative purposes or so we can feel good about ourselves but to demonstrate His kingship. Through us God wants to change the world, heal the nations, and dispense His spirit of restoration, reformation, and revival around the globe. The spiritual direction of this world depends on the people of God. When God's anointed ones respond to His call and function in His power, the enemy has no chance.

As children of God who are also priests in God's kingdom, we have the high calling and responsibility of proclaiming the Word of God and demonstrating His heart to lost souls. The best sacrifice we can ever offer the Lord God is our lives (Romans 12:1). Giving our bodies, hearts, souls, and minds to God is the great sacrifice God is looking for from us. Doing that demonstrates a life full of kingdom purpose and enables us to do what God has called us to do. The enemy may try to attack our minds and hearts with thoughts that bring discouragement or negativity, so it's important to fill our minds and hearts with the Word and Spirit of God so we are purposeful and adamant in doing the will of God.

It is important to understand we can never be completely happy or find fulfillment in life without doing what we are gifted or commissioned to do by God. True fulfillment is found in doing what God originally designed us to do. Ask God to reveal to you your divine calling and purpose so you can channel your resources, time, and dedication into it instead of trying to be like other people. You are you, and God created you as an original with a unique gift so you can bring a unique glory and honor unto His name.

## The Dangers of Not Functioning in Your Own Gift

Functioning in an office you are not anointed in or called to can be dangerous. If you are not careful, you can lead the people of God under your care away from Him, or you can end up living an unhappy life full of hatred and resentment. In fact, it can even be physically dangerous to try to function in someone else's anointing, gift, or ministerial position if God has not commissioned or graced you for it.

Leviticus 10 tells us about Aaron's sons Nadab and Abihu, who apparently stepped into the office of priest without being commissioned by God. They offered to God unauthorized fire (sacrifice) and immediately fire came out from the presence of the Lord and consumed them. Nadab and Abihu's mistake was that they offered God a sacrifice He did not request from them. Today God may not respond by striking us with fire if we operate in an office He has not called us to and offer an unauthorized sacrifice to Him, but be assured that His grace, His covering, and His presence will not go with us or be upon us. God delights in empowering His people and giving them specific gifts so they can do the work He has assigned to them with extraordinary power and grace.

## How to Identify People Operating in Gifts That Are Not Theirs

It is easy to tell when a person is walking or working in an office or operating in a gift he or she is not called to. Here are a few things that will be manifested in their life:

- They have no reverence for God.
- They have no concern for the people they are leading or are under their ministry.

- They are bossy and always want to be served, not to serve.
- They are judgmental and critical of other gifts, ministries, and people.
- They have no compassion for people and no passion for the Word of God (no sound doctrine).
- They make enemies easily as they see everyone as a problem or threat to their throne.
- They seem secure outwardly, but inwardly they are extremely insecure.
- They are controlling and manipulative.
- They easily find faults and weaknesses in people so they can exploit those weaknesses to solidify their own position.
- They reject anyone who does not measure up to their spiritual standards or ideas.
- They don't care whom they hurt with their uncontrolled and ungodly words.
- They have no desire to develop and release gifts in others because they fear seeing others succeed or do what they do even better.
- They never preach what they hear from God but what they see and hear from people.

Some religious leaders of Jesus' day had this kind of holier-than-thou attitude. They looked down on anyone who did not live up to their traditional requirements of the law or way of life. They even threatened to kill anybody who threatened their religious ideals or the offices they occupied. Their leadership was not based on what they could do for the people under their care but on what the people could do for them.

Thus, when Jesus saw the crowds who had come to hear Him, He felt compassion for them because they were distressed and dispirited like sheep without a shepherd (Matthew 9:36). However, God had promised to shepherd them Himself (Ezekiel 34:11–16). Through

God's greatest gift to the world, Jesus Christ, these lost people were going to find a compassionate, gracious, patient, caring, and loving shepherd to lead them back to God the Father. This is why early in Jesus' ministry He quoted Isaiah 6:1: "The Spirit of the sovereign Lord is upon me, because the Lord has anointed me to proclaim the good news to the poor. He has sent me to bind up the brokenhearted, proclaim liberty to captives and freedom to the prisoners." The purpose of your gifts, ministry position, or anointing is to set people free. Thus, you will know if you are operating in your gifting and anointing by whether the Lord is setting people free through your ministry. Only people with the compassionate heart of God will see such fruit.

Jesus demonstrated to us how a person called by God and gifted by the power of the Holy Spirit ought to function in the kingdom of God. A person operating in His own God-given gifts will be full of compassion, love, and mercy and will not compromise the standards of God to accommodate the culture of the world. Jesus did not condemn the people He came to rescue, heal, and restore to God. Yes, He condemned the religious leaders for their hypocritical attitudes and self-righteousness because He did not come for the "righteous" but for sinners (Mark 2:17), but in His heart He had compassion and forgiveness for them too. Even when He was crucified, He prayed to God the Father for His executioners, saying, "Father, forgive them, for they do not know what they are doing" (Luke 23:34). When opposed and falsely accused, He did not call for the fire of God to consume His enemies. Jesus clearly was the right man to rescue the lost world.

If we are to effectively lead people to God by using the gifts God has graciously given us, we must model our lives around the heart of Jesus Christ. When we use our gifts or leadership positions with arrogance and pride, without consideration or regard for people, they become vehicles that steer people away from God. But when we use them with humility, compassion, love, and a deep desire to be a blessing to people, the impact they make is life transforming and everlasting.

## Using Your Gifts to Bless Others

Whatever gift(s) you have, God has given them to you to bless those around you and advance the kingdom of God. There is a unique spiritual gift inside of you, whether you have discovered it yet or not. That gift needs to be awakened and activated by the power of the Holy Spirit so the body of Christ can rise up and demonstrate to the world the loving heart of God. Is your gift serving others? Then start serving. If it is teaching, then start teaching. If it is encouraging others, then encourage people. If it is giving, then give to the work of God and to those in need. If it is leading, then lead with diligence. And if it is showing mercy, then cheerfully show mercy to people (Romans 12:7–8). Don't neglect your gifts, and don't be concerned that they are underappreciated or unrecognized by others. It doesn't matter whether people recognize, appreciate, or accept your gifts. What matters most is that you are functioning in them as God ordained. When you are bringing Him glory and honor through your gifts, He will lift you up and bless you mightily. Never try to convince anybody that you are gifted by God. Instead, let people discover you are indeed gifted by Him when they observe the fruit that comes when you use your gifts to bless others.

## Things to Remember as You Function in the Power of Your Gifts

To begin functioning in your gifts and be used powerfully by God as a blessing to the body of Christ and those around you, you should keep some things in mind. First, you must dedicate your life to Jesus Christ, to His teachings, and to prayer. In doing so you will cultivate the gifts of God in you and more fully understand their purpose in your life so you can use them to glorify God and edify His people. Praying and studying the Word of God empower you to step out and do the work of God. They also help you discover the heart of Jesus and His passion for lost souls so you can imitate Him and use your gifts to bring spiritual freedom to people. This is why the Holy Spirit has graciously given you these gifts: to set the captives free and to illustrate the kind of God you serve.

Second, you must purpose in your heart to develop your gifts and use them at any given opportunity, big or small. If no opportunity arises for you to showcase the gifts of God within you, then create opportunities by finding people to bless. Embrace the gifts God has given you, and tend to them by reading books or watching programs that nurture your gifts so you can be the best at what God has anointed you to do. Again, don't aspire to be someone else. Ephesians 4:7 tells us God has given each one of us a special gift through the generosity of Christ. You have a special gift or blend of gifts, an exceptional gift the world is waiting for.

In the next chapter we will talk more about gifts and how to awaken the fire of God within you.

# Chapter 6

# AWAKENING THE FIRE OF GOD WITHIN YOU

Fanning into Flame the Gift of God

Paul wrote, "Therefore, I remind you to keep ablaze the gift of God that is in you through the laying on of my hands" (2 Timothy 1:6). Paul was reminding and encouraging his student Timothy to keep ablaze the gift of God that had been imparted to him. This is because any gift left unused is subject to ineffectiveness and slowly loses its fire. Most people in the body of Christ have little or no passion and zeal to do anything for the kingdom of God because the fire of their gifts and callings has burned out or been quenched by life's challenges and obstacles. Challenges such as persecution or rejection lead many men and women, young and old, to give up on their dreams and stop using their gifts effectively.

It takes persistence, determination, and faith to push through anything that threatens to stop you from using your gift to the glory of God. Persistence, determination, and faith come by standing on the Word of God and actively responding to it by doing what God commands you to do. Without igniting your passion for the Word of God, for Jesus Christ, and for the kingdom of God, you cannot push through life's obstacles and hindrances and be all God is calling you to be today.

Paul was calling on Timothy to keep ablaze the gift of God in him so he could fearlessly bulldoze his way through every obstacle and challenge and proclaim the gospel of Jesus Christ without being ashamed of his testimony about the Lord Jesus Christ. What has stopped you from functioning in the power of your gift? Is it sin, persecution, rejection, accusations, or suffering? All you need to overcome these things is to awaken the fire of God within you.

In this chapter our goal is to ignite or reignite the fire of God—the zeal and passion in your life—so you can live a purposeful, fruitful, and impactful life in Christ. Inside you reside the fire of the Holy Spirit and the light of the glory of God, which need to burn more brightly to the world so people can see Jesus in you and through you. It's time for anything that has suffocated the light of God in you or switched off His power in your life to depart in Jesus' name. You are not meant to live your life without God's power and without making an impact in the world. Through your gifts God has placed His anointing and fire in you for you to do wonders in this world, but that fire must be awakened first.

We need to do several things to awaken the fire of God in us and keep the fire of God burning in our life. That is what this chapter is all about. As Christians we need to understand that we are not powerless. God's power is within us. We must refuse to be sleeping giants.

**Refuse to Be a Sleeping Giant!**

As a young man I always wanted to find ways to help my family and improve our livelihood and help our society be a better place.

However, I felt powerless at times to do so. Sometimes when I tried, I was put off by those who had tried to help their families or society and had failed. Other times my own fears of failure and wrong thinking stopped me from trying to make a difference. I was too concerned about what the people in our community would say or think about me. My community in those days was not doing well, and few people had been successful, so when some stepped up and tried to be someone in life, some people would consider them to be prideful and full of themselves. This mentality kept many people, including me, stagnant in life.

This same mentality is keeping many Christians spiritually stagnant, passionless, and powerless to do anything for the kingdom of God within their local church or outside their local church. People are either directly or indirectly discouraged from using their gifts. Yet here we are as a church complaining that the church is powerless and ineffective. Well, the church is powerless and ineffective because we systematically view those who try to use their gifts or share the gospel or their faith outside the four walls of the church building as proud, arrogant rebels. Thus, those who are not strong in their faith and have no support from other Christians often give up or switch off their callings and gifts. This in return makes the church powerless because the church needs all the gifts "firing" to make a difference in the world.

Discouragement is one of the tactics the enemy uses to switch off spiritual gifts and put out the fire of God in the lives of people. And discouragement is especially devastating when it comes from fellow Christians and spiritual leaders. Many Christians are sleeping giants. They have allowed discouragement and criticism to stop them from using their gifts and from being everything God created them to be.

The day I personally discovered the fire and presence of God in my life, my passion and zeal to live a different life arose in me. My concerns about what others might think of me if I pursued serving God in ways unfamiliar to them died out, and all I cared about was what God wanted me to do for His kingdom and His people. This discovery changed my approach to life and the way I navigate it.

When you don't know how to differentiate the voice of God from the voice of man, you will fail to rise up in life and be the person God has called you to be. The voice of man most often tells you that you can't be or do certain things. Such advice is based on human experience. The voice of God, however, tells you, "You can do all things and be all you desire to be through My strength."

Many young men and women of God are sleeping giants, not because they desire to be that way but because they have listened to people who told them to shut up and sit down. If they tried to do anything in life, they were called arrogant and prideful. The first step toward igniting the fire of God within you is to refuse to be a sleeping giant. Do not allow the spiritual condition of your environment to dictate your relationship with God and how you respond to His call on your life. Doing things to glorify and honor God alone should be your goal and desire, not pleasing man or seeking his praise. Your gifts belong to God and must be used for Him alone.

Satan's goal is to stop Christians from burning with a zeal and passion for Jesus Christ and His kingdom. He wants believers in Christ to become lukewarm because he knows a lukewarm people cannot effectively do the work of God's kingdom. What makes most of us unresponsive to the Spirit of God and spiritually lukewarm is our failure to fan into flames the gifts of God within us. As a result, we join a status-quo Christianity of doing nothing.

Jesus did wonders in His life here on earth because He was zealous for the things of God. The fire of the Holy Spirit burned within Him and constantly fueled His passion and love for lost souls, the sick, the blind, and the hurting. He refused to be discouraged or stopped by religious leaders who had no interest in the people under their care. In the face of opposition, His zeal, passion, and fire for God kept Him going. Even as He was dying on the cross, He maintained His passion for the lost, so that when the dying thief next to Him said, "Remember me when You come into Your kingdom" (Luke 23:42), Jesus assured him, "You will be with Me in Paradise" (verse 43).

Nothing could put out the fire of God burning inside Jesus Christ. And when you have the fire of God burning inside you, nothing can stop you from doing exploits for the kingdom of God and fulfilling your God-given dreams in life. People who have the fire of God never quit. They never give up and never surrender because they have already surrendered their soul, mind, and heart to Jesus Christ, and there is nothing more to surrender. It was because of the fire of God in him that Paul declared, "For me to live is Christ, and to die is gain" (Philippians 1:21).

We need more than just knowledge about God. We need the very fire of God emanating from His presence to give us boldness and passion to proclaim the oracles of the kingdom of God and to continue living for God. Furthermore, it is the fire of God in us that gives us the faith to believe God beyond any reasonable doubt—even in the face of death.

The question now is how we can ignite or awaken the fire of God within us and keep it burning continually as we serve and live for Jesus Christ. Many people are on fire during a revival conference or Sunday morning in a church service, but when Monday comes they are as cold and spiritually frozen as ice taken straight from a freezer. What happened? Somehow Satan crept into their hearts, spirits, and minds and brought discouragement, hatred, and bitterness that quenched the fire.

## Awakening the Fire of God within You

When you were born again by the Spirit of God, the Holy Spirit of God kindled a fire inside you so you could continually burn with a passion for God and have the strength of God to do His will and demonstrate in your life the true character and nature of God and His kingdom here on earth. Thus, when you first surrendered your life to Jesus Christ, you were passionate, dedicated, and determined to study the Word of God, pray, and fellowship with other believers. You desired spiritual things. You wanted to learn more about God and His ways and nourish your spirit. Consequently, your spiritual light was shining more brightly every day, and Satan could not come close to you because of the power of the light of God in you.

This is why Satan continuously attacks you, using various channels to try to put out the fire of God in you. If Satan succeeds in his efforts, he will take away your zeal for Jesus Christ. And when your zeal for God's kingdom is taken away, you will find it easy to compromise, doubt God, and become careless about the things of God.

Sadly, many Christians today are no longer dedicated, passionate, or zealous for the things of God as they used to be because the enemy has quenched their fire through rejection, persecution, and offense. Without the fire of God burning in us, we are nothing but a religious and powerless people. Dead religion is dead because of the absence of the fire of the Holy Spirit. God is not satisfied with our being religious and powerless; He wants us to walk and live in His power through the Holy Spirit so He can bring transformation to us and through us.

So how can you ignite and keep the fire of God burning in you? The Bible suggests six things you need to do.

*Honor God in All You Do*

When your heart, mind, and soul are aligned with the heart and Spirit of God, you honor Him and show reverential fear for Him. And when you honor Him, His power is demonstrated in a mighty way in your life (see Daniel 3). Living a life that honors God is key to awakening His power in your life. When God is honored, He shows up in the power of His love, mercy, and grace.

How can you honor God? First, you must cast out the spirit of familiarity with God. In Mark 6:5 we are told that Jesus could not do many miracles in His hometown of Nazareth except lay His hands on a few sick people and heal them. The problem with the people of Nazareth was that they had "the spirit of familiarity." They had known Him since He was a child; so instead of receiving Him, they asked each other, "Isn't this the carpenter's son? Isn't His mother's name Mary, and aren't His brothers James, Joseph, Simon and Judas?" (Matthew 13:55). By asking those questions they lowered Jesus to the level of a regular person, which made it difficult for them to honor Him for who He was and receive His blessings. The spirit of familiarity with God lowers God to our worldly standards, which blinds us to His ways and prevents our spirits from receiving from Him. Honor God with everything you are and have, and He will spark a fire inside you that can never be quenched.

*Give Thanks to God*

When you give thanks to God continuously (Ephesians 5:20), even when things are not in your favor, the Spirit of God comes down like a rushing wind and awakens your faith in God. And when your faith in God is awakened, nothing can distract you from pursuing the kingdom of God with all your heart. When you are going through a difficult season in your life, instead of complaining or getting upset, give thanks to God—not because of what you are going through but because God can turn any bad situation into something good for those who love Him and have been called according to His purpose (Romans 8:28). When you spend your time crying and complaining about the injustices done against you, you lose focus on God's purpose for your life, and your passion to move forward in the Lord is affected. Giving thanks to God keeps your mind at peace and your spirit calm and connected to the Spirit of God.

*Place Your Faith in Jesus Christ, No Matter How Bad Your Circumstance May Be*

Every difficult circumstance in life can potentially disconnect us from God by raising doubts. Doubt causes many people to abandon God and even question His power or existence. Doubt puts a limitation on the power of God and on what He can do for you because it switches off your fire for Him. When you doubt God, you effectively abandon your zeal or passion for Jesus Christ and His kingdom. Faith is magnificent because it lights up our passion for Jesus Christ and kindles a fire within us for the things of God.

Faith also increases and maximizes the power of God in your life. This is why Satan constantly seeks to raise doubt—the opposite of faith—in your mind. Faith is critical to your dedication, stability, and obedience to live for the kingdom of God. So trust and believe God regardless of your situation, and watch Him do wonders in your life and with your life. The greatest mistake you can ever make is to put your faith and trust in man to get you where only God can take you. People can disappoint or abandon you because they can constantly change their minds and thoughts about you, but God will never disappoint you or change His thoughts and plans for you. Place your faith in Jesus Christ alone—not in man, not in money, and not in your own wisdom—and you will stay on fire for God.

*Pray, Praise God, and Worship Him*

Prayer, praise, and worship are so dynamic because they keep us connected to the power of the Holy Spirit and ignite our love for God and our confidence in His ability to do extraordinary things in our lives. In Acts 16 we see Paul and Silas in prison, where they began to pray and worship God, singing hymns to Him. Suddenly a strong earthquake shook the foundations of the prison, and at once all the doors flew open, and their shackles came loose. Paul and Silas had refused to let their fire for God be quenched because they were in prison and being mistreated. They kept their strong faith and trust in Him. Instead of complaining, they offered their prayers and praise to God, and God showed up in a mighty way. Prayer and praise and worship ignite the fire of God in us. When you are faced with difficult challenges, pray and glorify the name of God through praise and worship, and He will manifest His greatness in your situation. Never panic; just pray, worship, praise God, and wait on Him. In doing so, you will keep the fire of your faith and of the Spirit of God burning in your life.

*Stand on the Word of God*

The Word of God is a living word, full of life, active, and sharper than any double-edged sword, cutting between soul and spirit, joints and marrow, and discerning the thoughts and intentions of the heart (Hebrews 4:12). Only the Word of God can awaken your spirit to the Spirit of God and empower you to stand firm in any storms of life. Furthermore, the Word of God is the only word that can keep you moving forward in the Lord and faithfully serving Him. Too many people are spiritually dead, unstable, and unfruitful because they have turned away from God's Word and turned to the words of men and the pursuit of material things. Only through the Word of God can you find true life and activate the power of God within you. God is trustworthy because when He speaks and His word goes out from His mouth, it does not return to Him void; it accomplishes what He desires and achieves its purpose (Isaiah 55:11). Give your heart and ears to the Word of God alone, and you will stay on fire for Him in all seasons.

*Worship God with Other Believers in Christ*

Hebrews 10:25 tells us we are to promote love and good works, "not abandoning or neglecting our worship meetings, as some habitually do, but encouraging each other." Worshipping God with other believers will build you up and motivate you to continually follow Jesus Christ and pursue His kingdom. When believers in Christ worship God together in love and unity, the combined power of all sparks in us a deeper desire to live for God and motivates us to continually burn with a passion for the Word of God and to love God and people.

The enemy has deceived some people into believing they don't need the local church. Being part of the local assembly of believers is critical to keeping your fire for God burning. Never disconnect yourself from the body of Christ, as many people are currently doing. Stay in and with the body of Christ so you can grow and mature in the things of God. Find a place of worship that has the Spirit of God, the heart of God, and the love of God. This is important because your spirit can thrive, grow, and mature only in an atmosphere that accurately reflects the loving character and nature of God. Healthy and fruit-producing plants thrive only in the proper environment. If you place a plant in an environment that is harsh and has no oxygen, it will not survive. The same is true with your spiritual life—for it to thrive, bear fruit, and be healthy, it must have an atmosphere full of love, the Word of God, and the Spirit of God. Do not let past negative experiences keep you away from fellowshipping and serving God with other believers.

## Rekindle the Fire of God through Faith, and Flourish in Your Gift

While we have already spoken about faith, let's explore further its central role in keeping the fire of God burning in your life and your gifts flourishing so you can reach your maximum potential in the Lord. Our spiritual journey and walk with the Lord must confront many obstacles and challenges. If not overpowered by the power of faith, those hurdles can stop you from entering the destiny God has set for you. Faith in God and in the Word of God fuels your strength, purpose, stability, and determination to move forward in life and not give up when faced with difficult circumstances. Unbelief, or lack of faith, will take away your passion, purpose, and will to develop your gift and use it mightily to the glory of God.

In many cases, when we consult with others about what we desire to be or do, their response is "No, you can't." Because of this, many people are discouraged or try to enter their destiny full of the spirit of unbelief and doubt. Unbelief and doubt are holding many people back from exercising the authority and power they have in God through their gifts and from pursuing their destiny in Christ. The day I overcame the spirit of unbelief and doubt was the day I was born anew and afresh and stepped out in faith and trusted God to do wonders in and with my life. Today I can testify that thousands of people have come to know the Lord through the gift of evangelism God anointed me with.

When you cast aside all your doubts and overcome the spirit of unbelief, you will rekindle the fire of God in you through faith. You will flourish in your gifts and be a channel through whom God can transform lives and empower them to take over the nations with the good news of the kingdom of God. It is important to understand that before God can do what He wants to do with your life, you need to overcome unbelief, fear, doubt, and a man-pleasing spirit. We overcome unbelief by trusting God's Word regardless of opposition or persecution or other obstacles we might face and by being doers of God's Word. The Bible says, "Don't just listen to God's word. You must do what it says. Otherwise you are only fooling yourselves" (James 1:22 NLT). You must respond to the Word of God by doing what it says you ought to do. If God's Word says "go," then go, and God will take care of the rest, providing all you may need along the way.

Too many people are waiting for affirmation from man, and if they don't get it they don't think they can do anything for the kingdom of God. Affirmation is good, but it must come *after* you have already stepped into your calling and started doing what you should be doing. True affirmation that causes our hearts to burn with the fire of God comes from the Holy Spirit because it is the Holy Spirit who gives us our gifts. No human being can give another human being a spiritual gift. The Bible tells us the Holy Spirit distributes the gifts of the Spirit (1 Corinthians 12:11). He alone decides which gifts each person should have. If you are called to evangelism, you don't have wait to share the gospel of Jesus Christ with other people. In fact, a true evangelist is always looking for an opportunity to share the gospel. Fear of man and of the unknown causes people to have unresponsive hearts and to neglect their gifts so they can't function in the body of Christ. Consequently, today we have a dysfunctional community of believers who are not letting God manifest His power or life through them by using their gifts. The spirit of apathy and lethargy is dominant nowadays in the body of Christ because of fear. The power of faith in God—in who He is and in His ability to protect us and to watch over us—can transform us into courageous and bold men and women of God.

The time has come to set your heart ablaze with the Spirit of God and rise up in faith to do the work of the kingdom of God. It is time to get rid of an unresponsive and stony heart and respond to the kingdom call: "Go into all the world and proclaim the gospel to the whole creation" (Mark 16:15 ESV). The world is waiting for the true children of God to bring the healing rain of God into the broken hearts of people and show the world they serve a loving, caring, powerful and yet tenderhearted God. Instead of complaining about what has not happened in your life or what has been done against you, take up your position in prayer, intercession, praise, and worship, and seek the face of God. God will revive and lead you to your kingdom purpose. God is waiting on you so He can fulfill all His promises in your life. Stir up your gift, shake off unbelief, let go of your fears, and let God take over your mind and Spirit through His Word. Then watch your heart burn with a passion for the kingdom of God and flourish in all you do and desire to do.

**The Benefits of Responding to God in Faith**

God answers our prayers when we respond to Him in faith. When we call on Him and cry out to Him, He turns His ears toward us, hears our cry, and responds in a miraculous way. But too often we just wait without stepping out in faith. We wait for the right moment before we do anything for God, and in the process we miss many opportunities to serve God and to see Him work. True faith in God does not wait for the right moment but rather creates the right moment.

The reason many people are stuck in life is because they won't begin doing something where they are. They are waiting for a big opportunity, which in most cases doesn't come to pass. The bigger opportunities come only after we are groomed and prepared for them over time and as we operate in our gifts. Many of the miracles of healings Jesus performed in the Gospels came when people reached out to Him in desperation or when the sick were brought to Him with a sense of urgency. In places like His hometown, where the people had no sense of urgency and were full of the spirit of familiarity, Jesus performed only a few miracles. Jesus was nothing special in their eyes; consequently, they had no sense of urgency and could not respond to Him in faith.

Desperation leads to urgency, and urgency generates unshakable faith. Where there is unshakable faith, we see God's miracles. A lack of desperation and honor leads to unbelief. Where there is unbelief, it is impossible to see the power of God at work or to experience His presence.

The benefit of responding to the Word of God in faith is that our spirits will be enriched, empowered, and motivated to step out into our destiny. Faith will always lead us to our destiny despite a turbulent journey because faith in God always overcomes. Faith is beneficial to us because it keeps us purposeful, focused, and on track, and it helps us have a vision in life. Doubt takes all that away from us.

Please remember too that faith is not only for receiving material things from God. It is needed not just when you are going through a difficult season. Faith is for your everyday walk and fellowship with God. You must walk by faith and not by sight in all seasons.

## Your Faith Will Fuel Your Dedication to the Kingdom of God

In today's world it is not easy to maintain the fire of God within us. There are so many discouraging things happening both within the body of Christ and outside the church that many have lost their passion for Jesus Christ and His kingdom. A great number of Christians have lost interest in the things of God because of some bad experience they have encountered in the world or in the church. True soldiers of faith, however, do not give up on their kingdom assignment because of persecution, rejection, or some other negative experience. They do not allow anything to stop them from marching toward their kingdom prize because their dedication to serve Jesus Christ is fueled by the power of unshakable faith. As a good soldier of Jesus Christ (2 Timothy 2:3), you must continue to fight a good fight of faith (1 Timothy 1:18) regardless of the challenges or suffering you may have to endure.

The true Christian lives a life of *total commitment, total surrender,* and *total dedication* to the kingdom of God. Without unshakable faith, it is impossible to live such a life because the enemy uses so many things in the world today to quench the fire and love for God in the hearts of the redeemed. Every day the enemy tries his best to pull people away from God's presence, from serving Him, from demonstrating His awesome nature, and from pursuing His kingdom. Satan's goal is to kill, destroy, and lead people astray and away from the presence of God. But he fears passionate and dedicated soldiers of faith who refuse to doubt or question the power of God. Christians who burn with a kingdom fire and are sold out to the gospel of Jesus Christ can never be deceived by Satan's lies because their faith and trust in Jesus Christ are sealed. Whether Jesus performs a miracle in their lives or not, they will follow Him and live for Him at all cost because their love for and dedication to Him are not founded on miracles, money, or material things but on the goodness and mercy of Jesus Christ for setting them free from the prison of sin and death.

May your faith in God be the fuel within that causes you to fearlessly move forward in life and fulfill your kingdom assignment. But remember that to awaken the fire of God within you, you will need your mind, heart, and spirit connected to and aligned with the Spirit of God. When that is the case, your life will flow with passion and dedication for God. You will serve Him not because of people or for people but because of what the Lord God has done in your life. Dedicate your mind, soul, body, heart, and spirit to the Holy Spirit, and your faith will burn like an unstoppable forest fire.

Faith in Jesus Christ produces a thirst and desire for the Word of God and His kingdom. It produces immovable loyalty, commitment, and dedication to God regardless of outward circumstances. The Bible describes many people who had what we can call "unquenchable fire" for God because their faith produced a passion for the living and almighty God. People like Daniel, Shadrach, Meshach, Abednego, Paul, and, of course, Jesus come to mind. All had a fire for God and for His kingdom that Satan could not quench, even at the point of death.

In our day many Christians fall apart with just a single attack by the enemy. One assault from the enemy puts out their fire for and loyalty to God. Believers today don't seem to have the stamina needed to withstand the attacks of the enemy or the same fire or passion for God as the men of God mentioned above. Consequently, many churches have become social clubs instead of places where God manifests Himself in power and tangible anointing to transform, empower, and give life to the lifeless and hope to the hopeless.

Has God changed? Why don't we have the same power and determination that some of the people of God in the Bible had? What is the secret to walking in the power of God's anointing in a world that is spiritually dead? How can we have a true fire, passion, and zeal for God and maintain it while living in a spiritually and morally corrupt world? First, we must clearly understand that while people constantly change, God does not change. He is always the same, and He still wants to move in us and set us on fire for His kingdom. I want to help you discover how you can rekindle the fire of God within you and maintain it and function in it to bring glory and honor to God and win souls for Jesus Christ.

**Let Your Light Shine before Others**

As Christians, we are light and salt to the world and to those around us. The light of God is in us, and His anointing is upon our lives. According to our Father in heaven, we are like salt in this world, bringing the flavor of the Spirit of God on earth. In Matthew 5:13–16 Jesus explained it this way to His disciples:

> You are the salt of the earth. But if the salt loses its saltiness, how can it be made salt again? It is no longer good for anything, except to be thrown out and trampled underfoot. You are the light of the world. A town built on a hill cannot be hidden. Neither do people light a lamp and put it under a bowl. Instead they put it on its stand, and it gives light to everyone in the house. In the same way, let your light shine before others, that they may see your good deeds and glorify your Father in heaven. (NIV)

What was Jesus trying to communicate to His disciples here? Jesus was saying that a disciple who does not demonstrate in his life the heart of God and the values of the kingdom of heaven is like salt that has lost its saltiness or flavor. Salt that has lost its flavor is useless and cannot fulfill its purpose. Likewise, we who are disciples of Jesus Christ are effective and useful only if we do what God has anointed us to do. Mere religiosity or spirituality is not enough to build, uplift, transform, and help those who may be in spiritual bondage.

Along with being the salt of the kingdom of God here on earth, Jesus Christ also wants us to be the light of God. From the beginning of time, God's plan for His people has been for us to be a light to the nations (Isaiah 42:6; 49:6), spreading the light of salvation and mercy to the ends of the earth. In Matthew 5:14 Jesus reminded His disciples of the purpose and plan of God for their lives: "You are the light of the world." God's light in them was like a light placed on a lampstand to shine its light everywhere. The light on the stand was not to be hidden from anyone or be put under a bowl, which would obscure it and likely extinguish it. An invisible light is useless when we are in darkness. To see clearly in a dark place, we need to have a light. It is unfortunate that many Christians today have hidden the light of their gifts under the church pews and within the four walls of the church while the outside world continues to live in darkness. We condemn the world for being in such darkness while we lock our gifts and ourselves within our churches, forgetting that God gave us those gifts so we could unlock the world from the influences of the kingdom of darkness.

> Everyone who calls on the name of the Lord will be saved. [But] How then can they call on the One they have not believed in? And how can they believe in the One of whom they have not heard? And how can they hear without someone to preach? And how can they preach unless they are sent? As it is written: How beautiful are the feet of those who bring good news! (Romans 10:13–14)

Lost souls struggle to find their way into the kingdom of God because the light of the world and the salt of the earth (Christians) have hidden themselves within the four walls of the church. Indeed, many religious leaders are failing to train and release people to preach the good news of the kingdom to the lost. Sadly, this seems to be because they are concerned only about being served and growing their ministries, not letting others serve by going into the world. The world will not be saved without hearing the Word of God. As believers in Christ, we must stop condemning the world and the lost and reach out by igniting the fire of God within us and being the light of God by preaching the Word of God. Jesus did not come to condemn the world (John 3:17) or the lost because the world was already condemned by sin and in need of a savior. Jesus Christ came as the savior, the light, the redeemer, and the deliverer of the world and all those suffering under the kingdom of darkness. He shines His light and the glory and power of His Father in heaven on everyone who believes and calls on His name.

## What Kind of Fire Is Burning within You and Shining through You?

Our purpose as children of God in the kingdom of God is to shine forth the light of God Jesus has lit within us through the power of the Holy Spirit so that through us many lives can discover Jesus the deliverer, Jesus the redeemer, Jesus the life, Jesus the hope, Jesus the forgiver of sinners, and Jesus the lover of our souls. Is your fire for God and for His kingdom burning brightly? And what kind of fire is burning within you? Is it the fire of the Spirit of God or the fire of the spirit of the world? Many people today have *a* fire in them, but it is not a fire of God or a fire for the things of God. They have a fire within them that is full of the spirit of the world, and it is manifested in hatred, unforgiveness, bitterness, jealousy, envy, and division. The enemy has managed to quench the fire of God in many people's lives and replace it with the fire of wickedness and worldliness. Many people no longer desire the Word of God or the leading of the Holy Spirit. Rather than pursue God for who He is, they seek Him for what He can give them—namely prosperity. There is nothing wrong with believing God for prosperity, but when prosperity becomes the center of our faith, relationship, and fellowship with God, then we are in grave danger of being led away from God and eventually dismantled by the enemy. There is no doubt God wants to prosper us, not for our own selfish desires but for the expansion of His glorious kingdom.

Let God rekindle, revive, and Illuminate His light in you so your life shines and manifests His glorious goodness to those around you and makes you a channel through which salvation, deliverance, and kingdom life can be realized. The psalmist declared, "Lord, You light my lamp; my God Illuminates my darkness" (Psalm 18:28). The light of God is always connected or associated with salvation and deliverance. And where God's salvation and deliverance power are present, there is security. Where there is divine security, there is assurance that God will protect you and watch over you. Therefore, the psalmist declared that with God he could attack a barrier and leap over a wall (Psalm 18:29). When the light of God's salvation and deliverance is lit up inside you, you become fearless, passionate, and determined to step out in faith and use your gift to be the shining star of the glory of God to the nations. God's desire for the church and for every believer in Christ is to be the light of His salvation and deliverance. The fire of God's salvation must be burning brightly within us, and we as God's children must be doing everything we can through His power to see others experience it in their lives—that is our mission.

**The Breath of God in You**

When God formed man from the dust of the ground, He breathed His breath into his nostrils—*His breath of life*—and man became a living being (Genesis 2:7). It is crucial that we understand the power that lies underneath the breath of God because God's breath of life is not ordinary. It is extraordinary and powerful. It is a fuel that keeps mankind alive, and it is a fire that ignites our passion to do the work of God and to live as God originally designed every human being to live. By breathing His powerful breath of life into man, God graciously shared his DNA with us, making us powerful and dominant beings here on earth. Consequently, He commanded us to be fruitful, multiply, fill the earth, subdue it, and rule over the fish of the sea and over the birds of the sky and over *every living thing* that moves on the earth (Genesis 1:27–28).

Unfortunately, today many people have lost the authority or the fire God gave them because they have disconnected themselves from God's presence and turned to worshipping powerless idols made by the hands of man. Many others have contaminated the life of God in them by allowing Satan's lies to lead them into all kinds of sin. Sin of any kind is dangerous because its goal is to separate us from God, the source of life and all power, and when we are separated from God through sin, His power in us is disabled. Living a Christian life without the power of God is like a vehicle without gasoline—it can't go anywhere.

God has lit in you a fire through His powerful Holy Spirit to help you passionately live for Him and fulfill your God-given dreams and to equip you to unleash your gifts and talents in this world. The fire of God in you needs to be fanned into flame and nurtured daily with the Word of God so it burns away the chaff and brings life to everything within you. If you are born again by the Spirit of God, then know that you have the fire of God in you. The Holy Spirit makes you a powerful force in this world and a danger to the kingdom of darkness. The fire of God can cause you to stand strong and firm when you are going through difficult seasons of life, make you victorious over every scheme of the enemy, and empower you to fulfill your potential in life. Knowing all this, the apostle Paul commanded Timothy to fan into flame the gift of God that was in him so he could fully accomplish his kingdom mandate (2 Timothy 1: 6).

It is safe to say that many Christians around the world are genuinely crying out for revival. They want the fire of God to burn and bring life to the nations and to their congregations in a majestic way. Hence, they look up to heaven day in and day out, asking God to pour out His fire of revival from heaven. What they so often forget, however, is that God has already deposited His fire through His Holy Spirit in us and given us all we need in Him to succeed in life. If you are not moving in the fire or anointing of God, then you need to awaken the Spirit of God in you through intercession, praise and worship, and the Word of God and by doing the work God has called you to do.

## When the Fire of God Burns within You, You Can't Be Silent

Jeremiah, known as the weeping prophet, faced many challenges and obstacles in his ministry. But whenever he decided to quit and no longer speak in God's name, the Word of God in him became a fire burning in his heart, shut up in his bones (Jeremiah 20:9). Consequently, he could not remain silent but was compelled to speak God's words no matter how unpopular his doom-and-gloom message was. When the fire of the Word of God is burning in you, it doesn't matter who has rejected you, called you names, or abandoned you. Keep moving forward obediently, doing what God has called you to do.

Let God's Word in you fuel your passion to rise up and speak His truth in a world that has turned to false gospels. Even if you stand alone and have no support from anyone, do not be silenced from speaking the Word of God and living for Jesus Christ. As you walk with God and in God, let His presence set your heart ablaze so that through you people may experience the love, mercy, and salvation of our Lord.

Do you want your life to make a difference in the world today? If your answer is yes, then kindle the fire of God within you, burn with its compassion, passion, love, mercy, and grace toward the lost, and be the light of God that leads people out of the kingdom of darkness and into the kingdom of light. If you don't fan into flame the gift of God in you, then you will continue to wait on God in vain to do something in your life and in your society. And all the while God is waiting on you to arise in the power of His gifts in you and in the power of the name of Jesus Christ and do something about the spiritual condition of your nation.

## Chapter 7

# OBSTACLES COME BEFORE DESTINY

You Must Fight for Your Destiny

In chapter 1 we discussed briefly how obstacles can make us stronger. But if that truth is to be realized in our lives, we must learn to overcome the challenges we face. In this chapter we will learn how to overcome the storms of life and fruitfully live out God's plan and will for our lives.

The Christian life—in fact, life in general—is full of storms, challenges, obstacles, and opposition. If we don't learn how to navigate through life's challenges, we will continue circling in one place without reaching God's intended goal, plan, purpose, and will for our lives. Moreover, if we don't pull through the storms of life, we will be stuck in our old ways of living, thinking, and doing things and will be kept from God and His promises, presence, revival, and power.

If you rise above your obstacles, you will enter a place of spiritual fruitfulness and enjoy your destiny with God. But reaching your destiny in life does not come easily. You will need audacity, stamina, perseverance, and endurance. Above all, you will need unwavering faith, focus, and trust in God. When you place your faith in God, no storm can stop you from becoming the person God created you to be, because God is faithful, and He will make things happen for you. All you need to do is relax as you go through the storms of life, fully knowing that the God who called you is fighting for you, standing with you, and making a way for you to pass through the storm. To reach your destiny in life, you must learn to navigate the storms of life and conquer your fears. Fear is surely the greatest obstacle, for it causes you to doubt God, and doubt can lead you to discouragement. Discouragement can cause you to lose hope and give up the pursuit of your calling and dream in life.

## If You Don't Fight for Your Destiny, No One Will Fight for You

Again, in chapter 1 we looked at young David's encounter with the giant Goliath (1 Samuel 17), and we learned about the source of David's motivation and courage. Here we want to focus on another aspect of that story.

David actually faced two obstacles that day. One was the mighty giant who challenged the armies of Israel. The Israelites' destiny was on the line. If Goliath defeated them, they were going to become slaves of the Philistines. But David, though still a boy, trusted in the power of the name of the Lord, the almighty God of the armies of Israel, whom Goliath had taunted and defied.

The other obstacle David faced was the charge of his own brother Eliab. Eliab was furious when he saw his younger brother on the battleground, and he was especially upset when he heard David inquire about the prize that would be given to a man who killed Goliath. He said to David, "Why did you come down here? Who did you leave those few sheep with in the wilderness? I know your arrogance and your evil heart; you came down to see the battle" (1 Samuel 17:28). Now David's destiny also was on the line.

Eliab misjudged David and mistook his faith in the Lord for arrogance. Eliab's spirit is still very much alive among Christians today. Too often people who dare to step up to the plate and do something for the kingdom of God ... people who want to serve God with their gifts and are full of passion, confidence, and zeal ... are called prideful, arrogant, or egotistical and are classified as rebellious. This has caused many Christians to forsake their gifts and just sit in church pews doing nothing for the kingdom of God. Then they are called obedient and humble, but in the eyes of God they are disobedient for not using their gifts to advance the kingdom of God or to bless others. They are like the man who received one talent from his master and then went and hid the money in the ground (Matthew 25:14–30).

The spirit of Eliab has caused many gifted people in the church to give up on their God-given vision in fear of been labeled arrogant. Thus, they go to church spiritually silenced and overpowered already, with no life, no effort, no vision, no purpose, no hope, and no zeal for the things of God. We the church shamelessly continue to cry out to God to revive us, yet we have silenced the very gifts of God among us that generate the fire of revival.

There isn't anything humble about not doing what God has commissioned you to do. To set aside God's will to appease others is false humility. Humility is responding to the Word of God by doing what it says to do out of love for God and people and with consideration for others. Sitting and doing nothing or saying nothing isn't humility at all—it's a destroyer of your destiny. If you don't fight for your destiny, no one will fight for you. David refused to be silenced by his older brother's criticism. He refused to allow it to be an obstacle to his vision of redeeming the nation of Israel from the taunting Philistine giant, Goliath. He refused to allow his brother's words to stop him from doing what he believed with his heart: that he would defeat Goliath through the power of the name of God. He had to fight for the Israelites' destiny and for his own.

When you know what you want in life and know the God of all power and strength is with you, no criticism, opposition, or negative words can stop you. Too many people give up because they forget how powerful their God is. If your intention is to bring glory to the name of God, help others, and build up the body of Christ, you should never be discouraged by any storms of life that come in the form of criticism, resistance, rejection, and hostility. You must fight all those things to reach your destiny and fulfill your call in life.

**The Spirit of Courage Is Crucial to Possessing Your Inheritance**

When King Saul heard that David wanted to go out and fight the Philistine, he said to the young shepherd, "You can't go fight this Philistine. You are just a youth, and he's been a warrior since he was young" (1 Samuel 17:33). King Saul's words could have discouraged David and made him rethink his decision to challenge Goliath, but again David did not permit those words of fear spoken into his life to stop him. Saul's advice was well intentioned, but David's mind and heart were made up and set. His faith was in the Lord. David was not arrogant, but in his heart he was confident Goliath was going to fall. The king responded to David's courage and confidence by giving him a chance to prove he was the man for the job. Sometimes all people need is a chance to step out and do something great for their community and for the body of Christ.

It is wise to listen to other people and to seek their advice, but above all, your final guidance, direction, and decision must always come from God. What is it God has said you are to do for His kingdom and His people? What has God already shown you that you are to do? You must remember that your destiny and that of your family depend on your obedience to step out in faith and fight your battles through the power of God. Nobody can fight for your destiny; you are responsible to fight for it and to push through the storms of life so you can enter God's promises for your life. If you listen to the voices that say you can't, you are too young, you have no experience, you have no qualifications, or you are arrogant, prideful, and egotistical, you will never rise up and be all you are called to be. When you listen to God and know His will, you will act not only in obedience but also with courage. Be careful whom you listen to and what you listen to because what you hear will impact your life—either negatively or positively.

David's spirit of courage made the difference between him and the rest of the people present on the battle line that day. He was fearless because He knew the Lord and the Lord's destiny for him and his people. Because of his courage, it took David just one opportunity and one day to step out and solve the Goliath problem.

David's courage resembles the courage of Joshua and Caleb as recorded in the book of Numbers. Joshua and Caleb were chosen, along with ten other men, to spy out the promised land after the Israelites had come out of Egypt through the Red Sea and into the wilderness. The spies were to explore the land of Canaan to see what the land was like and whether the people who lived there were strong or weak, few or many. Furthermore, they were to learn whether the land was good or bad, unwalled or fortified, and whether the soil was fertile or poor. Then they were to come back and give a report on their discovery to Moses and the people (Numbers 13:1–21). All

*Discovering the Power of God in You*

this was to be done in preparation for the Israelites entering the land God had promised them.

After forty days of exploration of Canaan, the spies returned with their findings and reported to Moses and the people:

> We went into the land to which you sent us, and it does flow with milk and honey! Here is its fruit. But the people who live there are powerful, and the cities are fortified and very large. We even saw descendants of Anak there. (Numbers 13:26–28)

The spies who gave this report all saw the obstacles, challenges, and difficulties in taking that land from the giants and occupying it. By stating "We even saw descendants of Anak there," they were emphasizing the great challenge in taking the land. In fact, most of the spies thought it would be insane for the Israelites to even try to take the land away from those giants. The presence of the descendants of Anak instilled fear in the hearts of the Israelites and discouraged them from proceeding to take their future home (destiny) from the hands of their enemies. Thus, standing in their way to the promised land were giants (enemies), and until those giants were taken out, the Israelites could not inherit the land flowing with milk and honey promised to them by God. The choice was theirs to make. God had promised them the land. Now it was up to them to step out in faith and confront the enemies occupying the land and take it from them.

Caleb and Joshua objected to the negative report because they saw things differently from the other spies. They had a different attitude and spirit—a spirit of courage. Thus, they encouraged Moses and the people:

> We should go up and take possession of the land, for we can certainly do it … The land … is exceedingly

good … [God] will lead us into that land, a land flowing with milk and honey and will give it to us. Only do not rebel against the Lord. And do not be afraid of the people of the land, because we will devour them. Their protection is gone, but the Lord is with us. Do not be afraid of them. (Numbers 13:30; 14:7–9 NIV)

Why the different reports? Caleb and Joshua had courage because they trusted God. The other spies lacked courage because they depended on their own strength. The result? The people of Israel were so fearful and affected by the negative report given by most of the spies that when Caleb and Joshua encouraged them to go up and posses the land, the people threatened to stone them.

The spirit of courage is crucial if we are to posses the promises of God in our lives. Fear usually comes into our hearts when people we trust and respect tell us we can't do something, because we are not ready for that yet or don't have the ability to do it. Such words from trustworthy people instill fear in our hearts and prevent us from stepping out and trying something. Yes, it's important to listen to wise counsel, but how will we know we can't do something if we never even try? Show me a person who has never failed in life, and I will show you a person who is afraid to try anything new.

Fear is one of the most difficult strongholds to break out from. Its hold on people blocks the promises of God from coming to fruition. Many Christians have been held back from taking possession of the promises of God because they have been intimidated by other people and they fear what those people might think. So instead of possessing their inheritance or stepping into their destiny, they just sit and pray about it, year after year, without ever possessing it.

Why keep praying for your destiny when God has already given it to you and put it in front of you through His Word? Go out and take possession of it and then give God your thanks, praise, honor, and worship because He has given it to you. Are you tired of searching for your purpose in life? Are you tired of wandering in the wilderness, trying to discover who you are, whose you are, and what you are supposed to be doing? Remember: you are God's child, and through Him you can do all things because of His power and authority. Your future is in Him, so stop wandering in the wilderness of this world. Turn back to God, and God will reveal His purpose, plan, and future for your life and give you courage to lay hold of all He has for you. To realize your potential and use your gifts and thus step into what God has called you to do, you will need courage. Courage does not come by listening to negative, fearful, and timid people. It comes by hanging out with and listening to people who are full of inspiration, motivation, faith, the Holy Spirit, and the Word of God.

You need to have courage and faith before you can posses or reach your destiny in life because it doesn't come easily. Along the way to your destiny you will encounter Satan and his agents, who will unleash a barrage of challenges (storms) to hinder you from walking into your promises.

Jesus is our greatest example when it comes to courage. He was a man on a mission, sent by God to bring His intended destiny for every human being. Jesus too faced many obstacles from the religious leaders of His day and from the devil himself. His courage to do what His Father in heaven had sent Him to do was key to giving Him victory. Right after He was baptized by John the Baptist and God confirmed through His voice from heaven, "This is my Son, whom I love; with Him I am well pleased" (Matthew 3:13–17), Jesus was led by the Spirit into the wilderness to be tested by the devil (Matthew 4:1–11). But He overcame all the devil's temptations and immediately stepped into His mission and started preaching the message of the kingdom of God (Matthew 4:12–17). He refused to give in to the voice of the devil, who urged Him to turn stones into bread, to jump from the top of the temple, and to bow and worship Satan to receive all the kingdoms of the world and their splendor. Those promises of Satan were obstacles and distractions to Jesus' focus and mission, and He did not give in to them.

On your way to your destiny, Satan may offer you shortcuts (ascend to the top without building on the solid foundation of Jesus Christ), easy routes (give up on your calling), or fancy jobs and high-paying positions. These are schemes to distract you from entering your original kingdom destiny and assignment. Focus on the prize set before you by God, not by the world. Stay focused on your mission during temptations and challenges. God is faithful. He will see you through.

**Courage in the Face of Adversity**

To successfully reach your destiny, you must not only fight for it but also have a testimony and kingdom purpose. Many people struggle to reach their destiny and potential in life because they lack a testimony or something to stand on or cling to as they journey with faith in God through the storms of life. During the storms, instead of remembering the faithfulness of God and power of God and what God has done in their lives in the past, they see only the giant storm in front of them. Consequently, giving up seems like the only option.

What is your testimony? What has God done in your life? Or what powerful things have you seen God do in the lives of others or in those you read about in the Bible? Having a testimony in life can help you stand firm in the face of adversity and keep you on the path of pursuing God's purposes. Your testimony doesn't have to be dramatic to help hold you firm in a stormy season, and you shouldn't make up one or exaggerate it. Just look at your life now, and you will see the goodness and faithfulness of God upon it. That in itself is a major testimony. God has been faithful to give you the breath of life, and when you focus on that during the challenges of life, you will stand strong. Your testimony is crucial because it tells the enemy God is powerful enough to turn your mess into a message, your test into a testimony, and your tribulations into great triumph. When you are going through the challenges of life, don't see yourself as a victim or a failure; see yourself as God sees you—a victor. Through your testimony you can affect your life story, shape your future, and change the history of your family.

As we think again about David's encounter with the giant Goliath, consider the testimony David presented to King Saul. Remember: the king told David, "You are not able to go out against this Philistine and fight him; you are only a young man, and he has been a warrior from his youth" (1 Samuel 17:33). David answered with this testimony:

> "Your servant has been tending his father's sheep. Whenever a lion or a bear came and carried off a lamb from the flock, I went after it, struck it down, and rescued the lamb from its mouth. If it reared up against me, I would grab it by its fur, strike it down, and kill it. Your servant has killed lions and bears; this uncircumcised Philistine will be like one of them, for he has defied the armies of the living God." Then David said, "The LORD who rescued me from the paw of the lion and the paw of the bear will rescue me from the hand of this Philistine." (1 Samuel 17:34–37)

This testimony was enough to bring confidence to David and to stir up in him a strong faith, will, determination, and trust in the power of God to take on Goliath without a thought or fear.

A testimony of the miraculous doings of God, whether on our behalf or on the behalf of others we have known or read about in the Bible, is reason enough to have steadfast confidence in the power of God to save us, protect us, and help us conquer any giant blocking the path to our destiny, be it sin, opposition, rejection, or persecution. Your testimony to the greatness of the Lord is crucial to defeating all your fears, overcoming opposition, and achieving the goals God predestined in your life according to His plan for you.

What giant has been standing between you and your destiny? What obstacle is preventing you from experiencing the power and presence of God and walking in His strength? What stumbling block is stopping you from living out a fruitful and successful life that demonstrates the character of God? Through the blood of Jesus Christ and by the word of your testimony (Revelation 12:11), you can conquer any barriers and break down walls and curses in your life that hinder you from living victoriously. With just your testimony and your faith, you can revolutionize your life. Your testimony is powerful, and it can give you courage in the face of adversity because it reminds you of the miraculous deeds of God and His matchless strength and power. With Him by your side, no weapon fashioned against you can prevail.

In any battle we need courage, stability, perseverance, endurance, discipline, and a high level of focus on our target. Otherwise our enemy or enemies can easily defeat us. Through our testimony, the Word of God, and the Holy Spirit, God has given us a reservoir of power to fortify our courage, stability, perseverance, and endurance during a stormy season. The young David had courage, and the source of His courage was in the unmatched power of God. His courage and determination puzzled everyone around him, including King Saul, and it still puzzles many of us to this day. Courage is one of the missing ingredients in many Christians' lives today. Thus, many have no determination, perseverance, or discipline to remain focused on God or to pursue His kingdom and their calling in life. When opposed, most Christians withdraw and stop doing the work of God. And when criticized in the church, they abandon their spiritual gifts and put them on a shelf, as if ministry were to be performed only within the walls of the church. When we give up that easily, we are giving up not only on our destiny but also on those people God has called us to help discover their own destiny and purpose.

Standing between you and the promises of God are various obstacles. You must be strong and courageous. Don't be afraid of anyone except God, and don't be discouraged by opposition. Just stand your ground, for God is with you.

You have a kingdom purpose and calling in life. As such, you will face obstacles or challenges, but they should never cause you to give up. Just pray to the living God, who answers by fire (see Leviticus 9:24; 1 Kings 18:38; 1 Chronicles 21:26; 2 Chronicles 7:1; Zechariah 13:9; 1 Peter 1:7). He will answer your prayers and help you emerge victorious over your enemy. Your confidence to push through darkness and the storms of life must not be in your own strength but in the mighty strength of God. Our God is full of power, and His eyes are like a blazing fire (Revelation 1: 14; 2:18), so why fear man or Satan? If God is with you, who can be against you (Romans 8:31)?

Before the Israelites could reach the promised land, a land flowing with honey and milk, they faced challenges and made many mistakes along the way. They were short on patience and complained and turned to worshipping idols. Be patient with yourself, with God, and with man as you navigate the storms of life and soldier on to your destiny. Never complain (Philippians 2:14) or blame others for your mistakes or failures—take full responsibility for living out your own life according to God's plan and purpose for you. You are responsible for your own life and for discovering who you are in Christ and for achieving that. People and leaders are there simply to motivate you and guide you through your journey with God, but it's you who must be determined to seize your moment and live to the glory and honor of the name of God. No one is stopping you from becoming what God created you to be, and no one is stopping you from using your gifts—except yourself. It may be the way you look at yourself or the way you think. God wants to make you fruitful and powerful so the world can see His goodness and majestic power through you.

To be all God created us to be, God must be the center of our life … His Son, Jesus Christ, must be our Savior and foundation … the Holy Spirit must be our guide and strength … and the Word of God must be our only manual for living with God and others. One reason we don't win our battles in life, in both the spiritual and physical realms, is simply because we trust in our own skills, training, or background instead of in the name of Jesus Christ and in His Word. With our own wisdom or strength we cannot do much, but with God we can do the impossible. Jesus said in Matthew 19:26, "With man this is impossible, but with God all things are possible." And in Genesis 18:14 the Lord said, "Is anything too difficult for the LORD? At the appointed time I will return to you, at this time next year, and Sarah will have a son." There is nothing too difficult for our God. He can calm the storm, make a way for us in the wilderness, and lead us to the finish line.

It doesn't matter how long you have been on your journey. God is still God, and He can fulfill all His promises concerning your life, family, business, and calling. Never take a shortcut. Go through the main and only way, Jesus Christ, and enjoy your voyage no matter how difficult it may be, because at the end you shall rejoice and eat the fruits of your labor. No season lasts forever—each one has a beginning and an end. But our God has no beginning or end. He stands above our difficulties and assures us that our bad season is coming to an end and a new season is on the horizon. So rejoice and be happy in Christ.

## No Giant Can Stop God's Purpose for Your Life

Job said to God, "I know that you can do all things, and that no purpose of yours can be thwarted" (Job 42:2). If you are in God and pursuing His purpose and plan, you cannot be stopped by any person or any force of darkness. God is the one who made the heavens and the earth by His great power and outstretched arm, and there is simply nothing too difficult for Him to do (see Jeremiah 32:17; Luke 1:37). Remember the account of Joseph in Genesis 37:1–44:9? Adversity, hatred, imprisonment, and false accusation could not stop God from fulfilling Joseph's destiny. Joseph's brothers saw him as a useless and prideful dreamer, but God saw him as the Israelites' rescuer. Just because Joseph went through a bad time didn't mean his dream and God's purpose for His life were over. People have no power to kill or destroy the purposes of God in your life. If you have been going through a painful season, don't give up—God has not given up on you. God is a reliable friend who sticks close to those who dwell under the shadow of His presence (Proverbs 18:24).

Why do we sometimes lose our strength or spiritual momentum and struggle to step into our destiny in times of adversity? Maybe we have not found the purpose or meaning of our life in God alone. We may be trying to find our purpose in other people, money, careers, or ministry positions. When we fail to attain those things, our dreams come to a standstill. Perhaps we lose momentum because we don't have a purpose in life or know our kingdom destiny. Perhaps we are not pursuing God's kingdom and its agenda. When we don't know our kingdom destiny, we won't have a kingdom purpose in life. And when we don't have a purpose in life, we won't fight or stand up for anything. But when we know the destiny we have in God and know His plans for our life, our life becomes a journey filled with a godly vision, strength, and sustainability. If you are rejected or experience a setback, don't falter or give up on what God has called you to do. Rather, continue marching forward with an attitude of no retreat and no surrender to the enemy's lies, schemes, and arrows that are meant to destroy God's purposes and destiny in your life.

**Whose Purpose Are You Pursuing?**

Every person under the sun today is busy pursuing something or has a dream of some sort. The question is this: Whose purpose or dream are you chasing? Is it the kingdom of God and His purposes for your life? Or is it the things of this world such as material items, fame, or money? Fulfillment and true success in life are achieved by pursuing first the kingdom of God and all its purposes. In fact, it is only in pursuing the kingdom of God that we discover our own purpose and prosper according to the standard of God. Jesus said this to His disciples:

> The pagans pursue all these things, and your Heavenly Father knows that you need them. But seek first the kingdom of God and His righteousness, and all these things will be added unto you. Therefore do not worry about tomorrow, for tomorrow will worry about itself. Today has enough trouble of its own. (Matthew 6:32–34)

The unbelieving or worldly man is concerned—and worried—only about what he will eat tomorrow or whether he can achieve his own personal agenda. These goals do not benefit anyone around him.

But the spiritual man concerns himself with the purposes of the kingdom of God. He seeks to be a blessing to those around him and a channel through whom the character and nature of God are demonstrated to the poor, sick, and brokenhearted and to those held in the shackles of sin.

As He trained His disciples for service and taught about the kingdom of God and its mysteries, Jesus' goal was for them to discover their purpose in God's kingdom and go to the ends of the earth proclaiming its arrival and its goodness with power and authority.

Today Jesus has the same purpose and plan for us as he did then for His disciples. God does not change, and He has not changed His mind or plans concerning you. Have you been asking yourself, "What is God's purpose for my life?" The answer is to pursue Him, His kingdom, and His righteousness so He can reveal His nature to the world through you. And as you pursue Him, He will prosper you and give you a glorious future filled with hope and joy. Jeremiah 29:11 says, "'For I know what I have planned for you,' says the LORD. 'I have plans to prosper you, not to harm you. I have plans to give you a future filled with hope.'"

In today's world many Christians are chasing after money, fame, and popularity. I encourage you to chase after the kingdom of God and make God your only purpose and foundation of life. Pursue the things of God, and God will take care of all that concerns you. He will elevate you, prosper you, and use you for His glory.

## God's Purpose Always Prevails against All Adversity

Knowing your kingdom purpose and pursuing it is key to living a fruitful, focused, impactful, and successful life. Living without such purpose leads to frustration and living under the shadow of someone else's vision, plan, and goals. Whose purpose are you currently running after or advancing? Is it your own … another person's … or God's? Remember: only God's purpose prevails; man's purposes and plans are subject to collapse or change. Proverbs 19:21 says, "Many are the plans in a person's heart, but it is the LORD's purpose that prevails."

Run with the plan, vision, and purpose of God, and you will never be disappointed in life. Don't spend your life chasing after things that satisfy only the flesh. Chase after the heart, Spirit, and presence of God. And don't spend your entire life living out someone else's dream or purpose. Find your own in Christ, and own it through His Spirit so you can live a happy and productive life.

God has given to every one of us a unique purpose so that through us He can enlarge His kingdom influence and touch people in all walks of life. Furthermore, because God created us for a reason, with a specific intention, He wants each one of us to thrive in our gifts and be fruitful in every area of our life to the glory of His holy name. Consequently, it is important for us not only to know His kingdom purpose in life but also to own it. When we own our purpose, we will have a different attitude in life and a great reason to exist, and we will avoid chasing one dream after another. Too many people have a purpose in life, but they don't own that purpose—it belongs to someone else. People of purpose have a different attitude, spirit, and character. They are visionaries. They are dedicated to what God has called them to do, and they care about people.

Living with God's purpose in your heart empowers you to live a life of passion, determination, and perseverance so you can overcome all the stumbling blocks standing in your path to victory. When other people are giving up or are stuck, you will keep moving forward and thriving because God's purpose in your heart is burning and enabling you to prevail against any challenges. Kingdom purpose in your heart declares, "For to me, living means living for Christ, and dying is even better. But if I live, I can do more fruitful work for Christ" (Philippians 1:21–22 NLT).

When you are in God and pregnant with His plans, you don't have to fear anything because your only concern, focus, or desire is to release that which God has put inside you. Furthermore, if your motive in life is to do the will of God and please Him, you don't have to worry if man rejects you for doing what God has called you to do. God's purpose for your life will stand, and through you He will accomplish all He pleases with your life (see Isaiah 46:10). Stand firm, strong, and faithful in the One who has graced you to serve in His kingdom. Shut your ears to the voices of the enemy, which try to bring you down or demean who you are in Christ. Give your heart to the Word of God, to the Holy Spirit, and to men and women of God who teach sound doctrine, and you will never lose focus on what God has called you to do here on earth. It's only through the Word of God and sound doctrine that you can revive your faith in God and connect to His power.

## Connecting to the Power of God during Adversity

If you are full of faith and standing on the word of your testimony and on the power of the Word of God when you face opposition, you can achieve in life what no one else thought you could. When you are connected to God and His power and know God's plans for your life, no giant, storm, opposition, or criticism can stop the purposes of God for your life.

Briefly, let us look at how we can connect to the power of God during times of adversity and stay focused on the kingdom of God and what we are called to do in this life. In Acts 16:22–28 we find Paul and Silas facing adversity. Indeed, they were in prison.

> About midnight Paul and Silas were praying and singing hymns to God, and the other prisoners were listening to them. Suddenly there was such a violent earthquake that the foundations of the prison were shaken. At once all the prison doors flew open, and everyone's chains came loose. The jailer woke up, and when he saw the prison doors open, he drew his sword and was about to kill himself because he thought the prisoners had escaped. But Paul shouted, "Don't harm yourself! We are all here!"

Instead of complaining about being imprisoned, Paul and Silas had turned their hearts to God and connected to His power by praying and singing hymns to Him. God suddenly responded to their prayers and worship of His holy name by rescuing them. Knowing how to connect to the power of God during adversity is critically important. Being religious cannot help you in difficult times. You must know God and connect your heart, soul, mind, spirit, and body to Him through fellowship, prayer, worship, praise, and your testimony of Him.

Connect to God by thanking Him, calling on His name, proclaiming His deeds (having a testimony) among the peoples, singing His praises, telling about His wonderful works, honoring His holy name with joyful hearts seeking Him for His strength, and always seeking His face (see Psalm 105:1–4). Power to overcome adversity does not come by default or simply because we are nice Christians or churchgoers. It comes by connecting to God and developing an attitude of honor, prayer, and worship, developing a strong fellowship with God, and stirring His presence within through the power of the Holy Spirit and Word of God.

When you are connected to God, not only will you have courage and stamina to face all your troubles, but you will also hear the voice of God reminding you of His promises for your life—promises of His protection and promises of victory. In times of trouble, call to God (Jeremiah 33:3) and seek His face. Listen only to His voice through His Word and not to the words of those who bring discouragement.

Our spiritual stability, our dreams, and God's purpose for our lives can be disrupted by ungodly voices that whisper lies into our ears every time we are in a crisis or face challenges of some sort. In the next chapter we will learn how to hear the voice of God in a crisis or ungodly environment so we don't give up or give in to Satan's traps.

## Chapter 8

# HEARING THE VOICE OF GOD IN A CRISIS

The Still Voice in the Midst of Your Storm

In a time of crisis it is critical that you hear the voice of God. Otherwise you risk losing your focus in life, your sensitivity to the presence of God, and your dedication to what God has called you to do on His behalf. In a crisis it is not easy to separate the voice of God from the voice of the enemy or from your own voice or the voices of others—unless you are deeply connected to God through His Word. When you are, you can detect the Spirit of God and plow through any crisis because you have a target, a mission, and a purpose to accomplish with God.

God is still speaking today, and He wants to speak to you. However, if you don't know how to hear His voice, you will miss many opportunities God brings along your path, and more significantly, you will miss His plan, purpose, and will for your life. Moreover, if you don't know how to hear God's voice or detect His presence in a crisis, you will end up complaining and whining about everything. You will become shortsighted, unable to see the presence of God in your life and what He is doing in you even in the midst of crisis.

These are some of the important lessons and themes we will explore in this chapter. But first let us look at an incident that provides an excellent illustration.

In Luke 24:13–35 we are given a profound account of two men walking to a village called Emmaus, which was about seven miles from Jerusalem. This was on the day of Jesus' resurrection. As they walked, the two men talked to each other about everything that had happened to Jesus. They were troubled in their hearts that Jesus had been crucified. This was their crisis, and it made them forget that Jesus had explained before His crucifixion that He would be killed but on the third day rise again.

> As they talked and discussed these things with each other, Jesus himself came up and walked along with them; but they were kept from recognizing him. He asked them, "What are you discussing together as you walk along?" They stood still, their faces downcast. One of them, named Cleopas, asked him, "Are you the only one visiting Jerusalem who does not know the things that have happened there in these days?" "What things?" he asked. "About Jesus of Nazareth," they replied. "He was a prophet, powerful in word and deed before God and all the people. The chief priests and our rulers handed him over to be sentenced to death, and they crucified him; but we had hoped that he was the one who was going to redeem Israel. And what is more, it is the third day since all this took place." (Luke 24:15-21 NIV)

Cleopas went on to tell their traveling companion that those who had gone to the tomb that very morning had found it empty, and certain women reported being told by angels that Jesus was alive. Jesus suddenly spoke up, saying,

> "How foolish you are, and how slow to believe all that the prophets have spoken! Did not the Messiah have to suffer these things and then enter his glory?" And beginning with Moses and all the Prophets, he explained to them what was said in all the scriptures concerning Himself. (Luke 24:25–27 NIV)

They still did not recognize Him, but they invited Him to stay with them since it was evening, and He sat down to eat with them.

> When he was at the table with them, he took bread, gave thanks, broke it and began to give to them. Then their eyes were opened and they recognized him, and he disappeared from their sight. They asked each other, "Were not our hearts burning within us while he talked with us on the road and opened the Scriptures to us?" (Luke 24:30–32 NIV)

Jesus' death had dashed the two men's hopes that He was the promised Messiah, the One who would redeem Israel. But the reports from the tomb that morning sent them even further into the crisis. They didn't know what to make of the report of the empty tomb and the angels proclaiming that Jesus was alive.

We do not know why these two were prevented from recognizing the risen Jesus as He walked and talked with them. We know, however, that their minds were overtaken by what had happened, and they were discouraged because they could not fathom a suffering Messiah. Consequently they discussed these things, and when Jesus appeared to them, all they could do was share with Him their despair. Later during dinner He opened their eyes to recognize Him and then disappeared. When Jesus had first approached them, their hearts were filled with despair, discouragement, and disappointment—so much so that they could not discern the presence of God with them. Only when their crushed spirits settled down and they were at the table with Jesus did they suddenly recognize Him as He broke the bread.

The still voice of God can be heard and recognized only when we are settled in our spirits and have taken our minds off the pain caused by the problem we are going through (this does not mean we ignore the problem or pain) and refocused on the power of God and His Word. We can truly cast all our anxiety on Jesus Christ, knowing He will sustain us because He does not allow the righteous to be shaken or crushed by a crisis (Psalm 55:22; 1 Peter 5:7).

**What to Do When You Are in Crisis**

Most turning points in life take place during times of crisis. They bring us to a crossroad. At the crossroad, at that "make it or break it" moment, God wants to get our attention so He can reveal Himself strong in our life situation and show us the way to victory. The problem is that during a crisis we can easily become so wrapped up in what is going on in our life that we do not recognize God's presence or hear the voice of God and let the Holy Spirit lead us in the right direction. Thus, we make decisions based solely on our own understanding, wisdom, and feelings.

I have personally been in that position. I made the mistake of listening to my own voice and the voice of man and made some quick decisions based on my situation and needs at the time. Therefore, I gave up on a ministry I was helping with when another ministry offered me a position. But after a month or so of working in the new ministry, my position was terminated, and I was left in limbo. At that moment I said to God, "God, I thought You offered me that position." But the Spirit of God within me said, "No, you took that position out of your own desires and based on man's voice. You did not consult with Me and ask Me to show you My original plan, will, and purpose for your life." When I finally turned to the power of prayer, remembered the promises of God concerning my life, and stood on the power of His Word, God proved Himself powerful and faithful as He rescued my family and me and made a way for us to enter a new season of breakthroughs. With His provision I began serving God in my original calling.

From this humbling experience I learned a few things I would like to share with you so that when you are in a crisis, you can avoid making any serious decisions based on your own wishes, desires, or needs without consulting the Holy Spirit. During a crisis the number-one spot for you to be is down on your knees, praying over the situation and your life in general. It's when you are on your knees communicating with your Father in heaven that God unfolds His original plan, destiny, purpose, and direction for your life. Don't run to a person first when you are in trouble; run to God and not away from Him. Second Chronicles 7:14 says, "If my people, who are called by my name, shall humble themselves, and pray, and seek my face, and turn away from their wicked ways; then I will hear from heaven, and will forgive their sin, and will heal their land." When you turn to God in humility and prayer, God will direct your path and heal the "land" of your finances, marriage, ministry, or family. If you refuse to turn to God and instead turn to man as your source of provision or direction, you will continue to live in disappointment and without knowing the original plan of God for your life.

Here are some other important things to do when you are facing a crisis or stormy season: Turn to the Word of God, call upon God's name, calm down, sing praises to God, and focus on Jesus Christ, not on your problems. Never live in anxiety or in panic, and never fight over things you cannot control. You must leave those things to God so He can fight on your behalf. Just relax, pray, and worship God because your God is in control. Seek the face of God and patiently wait on Him, and God will speak to you and reveal His manifest presence. Finally, when you are in a storm, remember God's plans for your life and what His Word says concerning you and all His promises to you, and let that be the anchor of your soul and your faith in God.

In summary, when you are in a crisis or going through a difficult situation, don't panic. Don't turn your back on God, don't run away from the presence of God, and don't lose your faith and trust in the power of God and in His ability to rescue, protect, and watch over you. Stand still. God always shows up and shows the way out when we trust Him and refuse to doubt Him or give up. Great spiritual training comes when you are at a crossroad facing adversity. Adversity can't kill you if your eyes are on God and not on man; it will only make you spiritually stronger and more stable. So fear no adversity, persecution, or rejection, because God will always show Himself strong in these circumstances. He will prove to you that He is the master of the sea and Lord of all the earth.

## Don't Miss Your Opportunity with God Because You See Only Calamity in Front of You

We all receive opportunities in life to experience the presence and power of God, to thrive and excel in life and in our gifts, and to be the people God created us to be. What is so intriguing is that these great opportunities come mostly at times and seasons when we are going through difficulties—seasons of brokenness, loneliness, rejection, or pain and tears. It's in such circumstances that many people miss their opportunities to arise and shine with the glory and power of God because all they see in front of them is calamity after calamity—and no way out. Thus, they falter and close their ears to God's voice.

The Bible says, "Those who sow in tears shall reap with joyful shouting. He who goes to and fro weeping, carrying his bag of seed indeed, shall indeed come again with a shout of joy, bringing his sheaves with him" (Psalm 126:5–6 NASB). No matter how challenging your situation may be or how difficult people may make it for you, that gives you no reason to doubt the God who called you according to His purpose or to give up on what He has called you to do. Instead, you must continue, even with tears of pain dripping from your eyes, to sow seeds of God's goodness and seeds of God's mercy and forgiveness in the hearts of those who mistreat you. Then you shall reap with a joyful shout of God's provision. Psalm 30:5 reminds us, "Weeping may last for the night, but a shout of joy comes in the morning" (NASB). Don't miss your opportunity to thrive in and with God in the darkest hour of your life. With God and in God, you shall see the light in darkness and rejoice in His salvation.

When you experience trials or unpleasant moments, be careful not to say, "Why me, Lord?" or "I can't take this anymore," or to blame people. Do your best to turn to the Word of God during those difficult circumstances so you can hear God's voice, which is the voice of hope and a great future. Do not listen to your own critical voice or the voice of your troubles or of those who oppress you. Afflictions are only temporary, and they can produce in us an eternal glory that far outweighs our troubles (see 2 Corinthians 4:17). In times of calamity, when you turn to the Word of God you will see things differently and think differently. You will see yourself rising through the power of God, being empowered through His Word and prepared to be not only a testimony of God's faithfulness but also a channel through whom God can bring restoration and life to those who are depressed, oppressed, and broken by the challenges of life. In your darkest moment of life, God's desire is to speak to you and redirect you and empower you with courage to push through the darkness and enter His light.

## "My Sheep Know My Voice"—Be Careful Whom You Listen to in a Critical Moment

Disciples of Jesus Christ recognize that knowing His voice is extremely important, especially in these times when so many voices seek to influence our minds and hearts and pull us away from a strong relationship with our Master and Savior. If we don't really know how to differentiate the voice of Jesus Christ from the voice of the enemy, the enemy will turn us into a destructive path. To know the voice of Jesus Christ and be able to differentiate it from the voice of Satan or man in a chaotic atmosphere, we must first have an intimate relationship with Him, with God the Father, and with the Holy Spirit. Our relationship and connection to God and to His power are crucial during the darkest moments of our lives. In fact, one of the proofs that we are connected to God and have a relationship with Him is in our ability to hear His voice and be led by His Spirit in a critical season of our lives. Jesus said, "My sheep hear my voice, and I know them, and they follow me" (John 10:27).

If you are a member of God's flock, you are under His care, and you should be able to recognize His still voice amid your storm. Listen to what He is saying and respond by obeying and following His voice—which always leads to His life and protection.

The God who created you cannot abandon you or His plans and vision for creating you, and He can never leave you forever in the hands of those who oppress you. He will rescue you. As the old hymn says, "Turn your eyes upon Jesus; look full in His wonderful face," and all the things of earth—your struggles or failures—will grow strangely dim. All you will see is the light of God, the light of His glory.

Things in your life may seem to be at their worst, but that does not mean you have to entertain voices that say, "Give up. Commit suicide. Abandon your faith. You are a failure." In difficult moments, you need to turn to the Word of God so you can hear His voice for direction and encouragement. No other voice will suffice, so be careful whom you listen to or turn to for advice. If you listen to people who do not have the Spirit of God in them, you will be misled to give up on what God has called you to do. Always seek advice from men and women of God who are full of the Spirit of God and wisdom of God and have their minds set on the kingdom of God—people who have a burning desire to see others rise in the power of God and serve Him.

With the mushrooming of false prophets in these critical times, we must be especially careful whom we listen to. We must not fall for words that lead us to take shortcuts in life and to see God simply as a vending machine for miracles. Instead we need words that encourage us to develop our relationship and intimacy with God so we can hear His voice and be led by His Spirit. False prophets have turned serving God into a business and turned His church into a franchise selling miracles, holy water, and various other things at the expense of teaching the Word of God and leading people to a fruitful relationship with Him. To these false prophets, ministry is like a hobby, a job, or a cash cow. They forget God has given us a kingdom mandate to teach His people about His will, plan, and purpose and to communicate His voice and heart to them. These imposters have allowed their flesh to take over instead of trusting the Holy Spirit to lead them. They turn to witchdoctors or Satanism for power so they can predict what is going on in the lives of people and offer them solutions totally apart from the Word of God. Let us not give our ears or hearts to such people.

## Don't Listen to Your Flesh in a Critical Moment—Listen to the Holy Spirit

Many times when people are at a critical point in life, they try to come up with their own best solution to their problems. Unfortunately, in most cases they do so without first listening to the Holy Spirit and the Word of God. In fact, they confuse the voice of God with their own voice, which comes primarily from their inner desires—what they want to see happen, not what God has planned or is requesting of them. The voice of God does not speak more loudly in the storm or when people are panicking. He speaks when their spirits have calmed down and surrendered to His Holy Spirit. It is dangerous to claim that God says this or that when your spirit is consumed and overwhelmed by the troubles in front of you. You must first find peace with and in God and with yourself. Seek His face and surrender your situation to Him. He is faithful to turn things around for you. Responding to a difficult situation in your flesh has many negative consequences because the flesh desires what is contrary to the Spirit of God. It will lead you to ungodly actions and attitudes such as idolatry, sorcery, hatred, jealousy, and rivalries. But when you respond in the power of the Holy Spirit, you experience the love, peace, and joy of God (Galatians 5:18–22).

When we respond to difficult circumstances in carnality, we lose not only the battle we are facing but also the ability to hear from God and learn from the situation at hand so we can grow and mature spiritually. Another danger of responding in carnality is that we can mistake God's voice for our own voice and make deadly decisions that come back to haunt us. Then we blame God because we think He directed our decisions. The truth is that when God says something, His blessing is upon those who obey Him, and what He speaks always comes to pass. In Jeremiah 14:14 God told Jeremiah the prophets of that day were prophesying lies in His name, claiming that God had spoken to them and had assured them that the people would not see the sword or famine, for God would give them lasting peace. God told Jeremiah that He did not send these prophets or command them to speak such things to the people. They prophesied false visions from the deception of their own minds and not from the Spirit or heart of God. Instead of warning the people about their idolatry, the prophets gave them a false hope, and when Jeremiah prophesied the truth, the people didn't want to listen to him. In fact, they beat him up. The people of his day wanted to hear what their flesh desired and not what the Spirit of God wanted from them. We find ourselves in the same situation today—some prophets are prophesying to people that God is going to bless them even though these people are not even connected to God and are perishing in sin. These false prophets are not proclaiming, "Thus says the Lord, 'Repent, for the kingdom of heaven has arrived.'"

So many messages today center around satisfying our fleshly desires and getting things we want from God. There is nothing wrong with turning to our Father in heaven for provision, but if we desire only material things from Him, we have not understood His heart and desire for us. One reason we fail to hear the voice of God and see where He wants to take us is that our minds and hearts are filled with the things of this world. Thus, when we turn to God our prayers are centered on material things. That is why it's difficult for us to grasp the vision and plan of God. God's plan is not just to give us stuff. His desire is to speak to us and reveal to us His heart and master plan for the church and for the nations. When we seek His face and His kingdom first, the other things we need here on earth will be given to us. But those things are not number one. He is number one, and He is the One we are to seek first.

If we say God said something and yet we know deep in our hearts He didn't, beware. God will not be misrepresented, and He does not allow anyone to lie to the Holy Spirit. If He hasn't said it, we must keep quiet and patiently seek His face and His kingdom in humility. We must take God seriously and not play with Him! Hearing the voice of God is achieved by living in the Spirit, not in the flesh, because God is Spirit.

When God speaks to us, His people, He clears the way for us and opens the door for us to pass through into our destiny. The journey is not always a smooth ride, however. The enemy sets up traps to try to stop us from walking into our destiny, but God's purposes cannot be thwarted. Satan tries to stop us from listening to the voice of God and from learning the plans of God, but if we have indeed heard the voice of God and know where He is taking us, we can never surrender to Satan's challenges. We will continue to pursue the kingdom of God with or without money. We will not take shortcuts when the going gets difficult. Let us stay the course and go through the process, and God will be with us in that process. When we go through the process with God, we understand His heart both for us and for those He has called us to reach.

To hear the voice of God, we need to allow God to be our firm foundation and focus and to allow His Holy Spirit—not our flesh or our feelings—to be our guide. We fail to hear the voice of God when we make money or some other earthly desire the center of our spiritual lives. All we see and hear is what we want and not what God wants. May the Lord change us and transform us so we can love and pursue Him for who He is rather than for what He can do for us.

*Dr. Kazumba Charles*

## The Still Voice in the Midst of Your Storm

In 1 Kings 19 we read about Elijah being on the run after Queen Jezebel threatened to kill Him. Elijah fled into the wilderness. While there in the wilderness, instead of praying for God to protect him or rescue him, he prayed that he might die. He said to God, "I have had enough! Lord, take my life, for I'm no better than my fathers" (verse 4). Elijah was in deep depression. The death threats had brought a crisis in his life, and he decided he would rather die than continue to live. Elijah's desire to give up living because of the crisis was not unique to him or his time. When the going gets tough, some people today, both Christian and non-Christian, would rather end their lives than continue to live in a difficult condition. All they see is the storm around them. They don't see God, and they cannot hear Him speak words of deliverance and direction in the fierce storm. Human strength, wisdom, or power can take us a certain distance, but only God can take us to our final destination through His supernatural power. Elijah had had enough. He could not take it any longer because his strength could not bear the weight of the death threats. Yet in the power of the Lord, Elijah continued on into the wilderness until he reached Mount Sinai and entered a cave.

> Then the word of the LORD came to him, and He said to him, "What are you doing here, Elijah?" He replied, "I have been very zealous for the Lord God of Hosts, but the Israelites have abandoned your covenant, torn down your altars, and killed your prophets with the sword. I alone am left, and they are looking for me to take my life." (1 Kings 19:9–10)

Elijah's explanation of his presence at Sinai revealed that he was discouraged, in despair, lonely, and isolated. God commanded him to go out of the cave he was hiding in and stand on the mountain in the Lord's presence.

> At that moment, the Lord passed by. A great and mighty wind was tearing at the mountains and was shattering cliffs before the Lord, but the Lord was not in the wind. After the wind there was an earthquake, but the Lord was not in the earthquake. After the earthquake there was a fire, but the Lord was not in the fire. And after the fire there was a voice, a soft whisper. When Elijah heard it, he wrapped his face in his mantle and went out and stood at the entrance of the cave. Suddenly, a voice came to him and said, "What are you doing here, Elijah?" (1 Kings 19:11–13)

Elijah gave the same answer he had given before. Then the Lord told him to return the way he had come to the wilderness of Damascus and anoint Hazael as king over Aram, Jehu son of Nimshi as king over Israel, and Elisha son of Shaphat as his successor.

From this account we learn that God is still God even in the midst of our storms. When we are discouraged or in despair, He can reveal His presence, power, and future plan to us. Furthermore, He communicates to us with a still, small voice as well as through powerful displays of His majestic glory.

You may be going through a difficult situation in your life. You may be scared and discouraged because of what you are going through. You may even be tempted to think the only way out is to end your life, but that is the devil lying to you because in God we always have hope. All you need when you are facing difficult times in life is to turn back to God and seek His presence and voice so He can direct your path. God wants to communicate to you in His soft and still voice and reveal to you His mighty presence and master plan for your calling and life.

## Not Every Voice We Hear Is from God

It is important to know how to hear the voice of God because when we know how to do that, we will also know how to detect the Spirit of God and differentiate it from the spirit of Satan and of the world. Many voices are speaking or trying to speak to us to direct our lives away from God. The most dominant ones are our own voices, the voices of other people, the voices of the world, and the voices of the kingdom of darkness. We must recognize that not all voices we hear are from God. If we don't know how to recognize the still, small voice of God in difficult times, the enemy can mislead us into doing something that results in defeat. Today many are claiming, "Thus says the Lord," and instructing people to do things that are unbiblical. Numerous people are following them because they don't know how to hear the still voice of God for themselves during turbulent times. God's method of communicating with us has not changed; He still speaks to us through His Word, through other people such as spiritual leaders or even ordinary people, and through His Holy Spirit. If you don't know the Word of God, however, you won't know when God is speaking to you through His Holy Spirit or through other people. Knowing the unchanging Word of God is crucial to hearing the voice of God.

First Samuel 3 records the call of young Samuel. However, when God first called Samuel, the boy confused the voice of God with that of Eli. Why? We are told Samuel could not recognize the voice of God at that time because he did not yet know the Lord and the word of the Lord had not yet been revealed to him. In simple terms, no prior vision or voice of God had come to Samuel for him to be able to recognize His voice. Consequently, when God called out for him, Samuel kept going to Eli, thinking Eli was calling him. After the third time this happened, Eli figured out that Samuel had been hearing the voice of God. So Eli told Samuel, "Go and lie down. If He calls you, say, 'Speak, Lord, for your servant is listening'" (1 Samuel 3:9). From this account we learn that it is impossible to hear God when we don't know His word or if it has not been revealed to us. The great news is that God has revealed His word to us through the Bible. The Bible records not only God's word but also His voice to humanity. When we read and study the Word of God, the Bible, we are learning how to hear the voice of God. The Bible reveals God's purpose, plan, and calling for our lives. His Word gives us life, inspires our faith in Him, and brings stability in our walk with Him.

Do you want to know your purpose in life or God's plans for your life? Then you must turn to the Word of God first, because the Bible is still the way God communicates to us His purpose or destiny. Be careful what you give your ears to because many people are claiming, "Thus says the Lord," but God has not spoken to them. When God speaks, His word is always in line with His Spirit and plan for your life. In fact, His message leads us to love Him more, to do what He has commanded us to do, and to tell others about His kingdom.

Any words that lead you away from loving God more, living for Him passionately, and proclaiming His kingdom are not a voice from God. Voices that say you are unredeemable, a failure, cursed, and hopeless with no future are not from God. Just because people say no to you doesn't mean God has said no to you. Seek God in challenging times, and He will do greater things through your life than you ever thought you could do. One word from God can change your life and turn your dying situation into life once again (Ezekiel 37). Don't be afraid to question things you hear. Ask whether it is God speaking or someone else. Only the Word of God can lead you to the promises of God and your destiny, and only the Word of God can reveal God's plans for you. Before you do anything, consult God's Word and pray and seek the counsel of men or women of God who have a kingdom mind-set and are prayerful, full of the Holy Spirit, and dedicated to the Word of God and not to the ways or traditions of man and this world. People who do not know God's Word and are not dedicated to it will likely give you costly advice that can lead to disaster. Before you do anything, seek God.

In 2 Chronicles 18, King Ahab of Israel asked Jehoshaphat, king of Judah, to go with him to war. But Jehoshaphat said to Ahab, "First, please ask what the Lord's will is" (verse 4). Interestingly, when King Ahab gathered four hundred prophets to ask them whether the two kings should go for war with Ramoth–gilead, all four hundred told the king, "March up, and God will hand it over to the king" (verse 5). But did all four hundred prophets truly hear God tell them to give the green light to the king and assure him of victory? How could anyone disagree with so many prophets? After all, prophets were trusted and respected and honored because they were entrusted with communicating to the people the very words of God. With all four hundred prophets saying yes, one would surely agree that God indeed had authorized the king to go to battle—but He had not.

The prophets here may have acted based on their position of influence as prophets, or their past experience with God, or familiarity with His ways instead of truly hearing His voice. King Jehoshaphat, however, wanted another opinion before he would go with the king to war, so he suggested they ask a different prophet. The only other prophet was Micaiah, son of Imlah, but King Ahab hated Micaiah because he never prophesied what Ahab wanted to hear. Jehoshaphat insisted they ask Micaiah, and when they brought him before the king, Micaiah prophesied nothing but the word of God and declared impending disaster. He even warned the king that if he went to war he would not return alive. Ahab rejected Micaiah's advice and indeed was killed.

Just because ten people—or even four hundred—tell you to do something doesn't mean you should take them at their word. Only

God is to be taken at His word. His words are true and final and are all that matter.

As a disciple of Jesus Christ, you must clearly hear your Master's voice among the many false prophets who claim to speak in the name of God. The misleading voices of these false prophets can lead you into unending misery and spiritual confusion as you pursue the world instead of the kingdom of God. Countless people have given up on God and on their calling because they have listened to voices that are not from God and have no interest in seeing the kingdom of God expanded.

When the voice of God is spoken into your life, it sets you on fire. It ignites your gifts and your passion for the Word of God and causes you to arise to proclaim the good news of the kingdom of God. The voice of God can turn an intimidated person into a warrior and a fearful person into a fierce servant of God. If you are still confused and miserable and living in fear, consider whose voice you are listening to.

**Whoever Is of God Hears the Words of God**

Jesus said, "Whoever is of God hears the words of God. The reason why you do not hear them is that you are not of God" (John 8:47). One of the marks of true children of God is their ability to hear the Father's words. If you are a child in the house of the Lord, you should be able to hear God's words because the words of God are spirit and life (John 6:63), and they make you know the truth that sets you free (John 8:32).

Jesus Himself stated, "I can do nothing on my own. As I hear, I judge, and my judgment is just, because I seek not my own will but the will of Him who sent me" (John 5:30). If we don't hear the voice of the Father, we can't do anything of value in the kingdom of God. In fact, we can't judge any situation correctly or even seek and do the will of God. To make sound judgments or decisions, we need to hear the voice of God. To represent God and speak on His behalf, we need to hear from Him and communicate His message accurately. Without hearing the voice of God through His Word, we can easily misread Him and misrepresent Him to other people. Here is what you need to do to hear the voice of God in the ungodly environment of today's world:

- Read the Word of God and God will instruct you in the way you should go (Psalm 32:8–9). He will give you counsel with His eyes upon you (Isaiah 30:21).
- Dedicate yourself to prayer, praise, and worship, and God will speak His word to you (Acts 13:2).
- Repent of any known sin in your life and be led by the Spirit of God and not the flesh (Romans 8:14).
- Remove every hatred, unforgiveness, and bitterness, and do good—and God will hear your prayers and give you the desires of your heart (Psalm 37:3–4).
- Humble yourself before the almighty God, and trust in Him with all your heart. Lean not on your own understanding—then He will make your path straight and you will "find favor and good repute in the sight of God and man" (Proverbs 3:4–6 NASB).

There is a prominent teaching today that we don't need to repent of any sins we fall into. That is the devil's lie. Don't buy this unbiblical teaching because sin separates us from God, and if it separates us from God, then it will prevent us from having an intimate relationship with Him. Isaiah 59:1 says God's hand is not too short to save and His ear is not too deaf to hear, but our iniquities build barriers between us and God and make Him hide His face from us so He does not listen to us.

The extreme grace movement that dismisses repentance has led many people away from the presence and power of God and opened them to the influence of the kingdom of darkness. God's grace does not permit us to continue living in sin; rather, it enables us to come closer to God and to dwell in His presence and walk in His power without being condemned by our past sinful ways. Don't hide behind "extreme grace." The true grace of God gives us opportunity to develop a deeper fellowship and relationship with Him. Grace gives us a second chance to make things right with God and to correct our ways with Him so our spirit can reconnect to His Spirit as our Abba Father. It's time to reconnect with God, hear His voice, and live in His will so we can thrive in God's presence, produce much fruit, and reflect His glory and power.

## God Is Still Speaking Today through the Voice of His Word

Every time you read the Bible, know that God is speaking to you and giving you instructions on how to live for Him and with other people. He is also giving you insight into who you are in God and with God.

When we look deeply into the Bible, we not only see God speaking to His people of old but we also hear Him speaking to us. His Word brings correction and reproof and trains us in righteousness so we can be complete in Him, fully equipped for every good work (2 Timothy 3:16). Romans 15:4 states, "For everything that was written in the past was written for our instruction, so that through endurance and encouragement of the Scriptures, we might have hope." Whether in the Old Testament or the New Testament, God's instruction gives us hope in Him. Of course, not everything in the Hebrew Scriptures (Old Testament) applies to us today, but we still see God speaking there in ways that were different from the ways of the world and the false prophets. This can give us great insight on how to distinguish the voice of God from the voice of the enemy in our chaotic world.

The Bible is and should always be treated as—your primary source of instruction. You must evaluate everything you hear or are told based of the Word of God. First John 4:1 encourages us to test every spirit to see whether it is from God because many false prophets have gone out into the world. One way to avoid being misled by ungodly voices is to know who you are in God and what He has called you to do in life. When you have this assurance, you can't follow just anything that comes your way because God does not change His plans or purpose for your life.

Anything that takes you away from the will and vision of God for your life is not from God. For example, any voices that say you are running too hard for God and that you need to slow down so you do not burn out are not from God. Of course, when you were running after the things of this world, those same voices did not tell you to slow down. In fact, they didn't care at all. But now that you are running passionately after the kingdom of God, they are trying to slow you down! I would rather run hard for the things of God and burn out for Him, giving 100 percent to Him and His kingdom than give in to the tempting voices of the devil and those he uses. If you know how to rest in God and enjoy fellowship with Him by renewing your spirit with His Word, you will never burn out but rather continue to burn with the fire of God.

In the next chapter we will look at who we are in God and what God says about us so we can confidently obey His voice and step out to do His work regardless of what people may say or do to us.

# Chapter 9

# I AM WHO GOD SAYS I AM

A Redeemed Child of God

> Then God said, "Let us make man in our image, after our likeness. And let them have dominion over the fish of the sea and over the birds of the heavens and over the livestock and over all the earth and over every creeping thing that creeps on the earth." So God created man in his own image, in the image of God he created him. And God blessed them. And God said to them, "Be fruitful and multiply and fill the earth and subdue it, and have dominion over the fish of the sea and over the birds of the heavens and over every living thing that moves on the earth." (Genesis 1:26–28 ESV).

These verses are key to man's discovery of his identity and his source of authority and power. It is here we first discover God's intention and purpose for mankind: to be *fruitful*, *multiply*, and *fill the earth* and *subdue the earth* and *have dominion* over every living thing that moves on the earth.

People who are born of the Spirit of God are not just ordinary people; they are extraordinary in the sense that they possess the abilities of God. We can fully exercise the kingdom authority and power God has placed in us if we humbly yield ourselves to the Holy Spirit. However, before we can fully discover our kingdom power and function in it to advance the rule and reign of God's kingdom, we need to discover who we really are in the kingdom of God. When we resolve the issue of our identity, who we are in God's kingdom, we will easily understand what we are called to do as ambassadors of Christ and what our duties are in God's kingdom.

If the identity issue isn't resolved in your life, it is easy to allow other people to give you an identity that does not line up with the original purpose of God for your life. Moreover, if you don't know who you are in Christ, you will spend your life copying someone else. You will never be comfortable living in your own skin and you will not appreciate the family you were born into and the gifts God has blessed you with. Not knowing who you are in God and what you can do through Him can make you a fake, a person who seeks attention, tries to please others, and is easily manipulated by people. You will be led to pursue goals, careers, and dreams that are not ordained by God. This is why so many people struggle and continue to struggle in life. When you live by man's design, you will never be happy. Only when you live by God's design will you forever be happy and thrive at everything your hand touches.

One reason we choose to live like someone else instead of being the people God created us to be is simply that we are afraid to walk alone, to look different, and to be called names. We would rather join others than stand against them. If they are not doing anything for God, we too do nothing. But that is not who God designed us to be. He designed us to be different and unique so that through our uniqueness we can display the characteristics of God and impact the lives of people around the world. We make a grave mistake trying to find our identity through people or through our careers, titles, or gifts. Our identity cannot be found in any of those things—it can be found only in God, our creator. Through the Bible God reveals to us exactly *who we are* and *whose we are* and our *purpose* in life.

## Resolving the Identity Struggle

One of the greatest struggles people have today, whether they are in the church or in the world, is indeed the struggle for identity—to determine who they really are. The mind of man is filled with questions such as these: *Who am I? Where did I come from? What is my purpose in life?* These questions constantly linger in the minds and hearts of Christians and non-Christians alike. Finding who we are is crucial to finding our purpose, joy, happiness, and fulfillment, as well as our contentment and focus in life. Consequently, the moment a person is born, the journey to discover who he or she is automatically begins.

The unfortunate thing is that many of us try to find our identity in a job position, money, friends, our talents, or a title. Yet this only leaves us disappointed and unsatisfied because these things cannot truly identify who we are here on earth. Furthermore, we end up weary and exhausted chasing after all these things trying to find ourselves. Even if we succeed in these endeavors, we continue to search for more because we are not satisfied. Proverbs 23:4 gives us wise counsel: "Do not weary yourself to gain wealth, cease from your consideration of it" (NASB). True wealth and identity are found not in a job or money but in God and who we are in Him—redeemed children of the King of kings. Once we discover that truth, money, jobs, positions, or friends won't define who we are because we are children of God, period.

Another crucial element to understand here is that we cannot resolve our identity crisis by looking at ourselves through the stained lenses of our skin color, educational background, nationality, talents, gifts, or the people we hang out with. This is because we are not just physical beings but also spiritual beings, created by the spiritual God. Thus, to find who we are, we need to turn to the One who created us, God Almighty.

Many people struggle to find a group of people, a church, a workplace, or a community to live in or join, but they just can't fit in because they are different inside and out. To fit in and be accepted, they abandon who they are and try to be and live like everyone else. This makes them artificial, unproductive, and uncreative. They are afraid they won't be accepted by others in the group if they are different or unique, so they go along with the status quo. In the process they kill their gifts and talents, which could save a life or even a nation.

Jesus refused to give up His uniqueness and kingdom calling and join the religious people who had failed both God and His people. He came to make a difference, and *for Him to make a difference, He had to be different.* He had to have a unique spirit and heart. He paid a heavy price for that, as He was rejected, ridiculed, mocked, and opposed, but His impact and legacy stand today and will continue to stand from generation to generation. Don't be afraid to be different. Just be you, and let God shine His light upon you, and you will make a difference in the world. Jesus knew who He was, so He stuck by His mission without compromise.

When you know who you are in God, you won't compromise the calling of God on your life just to gain man's approval or to gain wealth or popularity because it doesn't profit a person to gain the whole world and forfeit his soul (Mark 8:36). In fact, people who have a kingdom purpose and call on their life often find they have fewer friends and support because they don't fit in to the world system and its traditions. The apostle Paul and the disciples of Jesus Christ were rejected, persecuted, beaten, and thrown out of cities because they had something in them that was totally different from the world. They had in their hearts Jesus Christ, the power of the Holy Spirit, and the Word of God. Jesus even warned His disciples that because of His name they would be seized, persecuted, put into prison, and brought before kings and governors. But He also explained that these events would be an opportunity for them to give their testimony about Him (Luke 21:12–13). When you are opposed or persecuted, you don't have to worry or give up on your kingdom mission or your identity in God. Rather you should see this as a great opportunity to testify of the greatness of the Lord Jesus Christ, who has redeemed you from the kingdom of darkness and brought you into the kingdom of light.

## Satan's Goal Is to Kill Your Identity in God—Don't Dance to His Music

Through his trickery the father of all deceptions, Satan, tried to steal, kill, and destroy Adam and Eve's true identity in God by offering them another identity. He offered them equality with God their creator, saying they would possess the same powers God did if they would eat the forbidden fruit. But if we look at Adam and Eve carefully, we see that they were already powerful, for they were created in the very image of God, and God had given them dominion over every other living creature on earth. Thus, Satan's offer was simply a gimmick to take their power away from them by leading them to disobey the instructions God had given them.

Satan likewise seeks to deceive us into forfeiting our identity in God by offering a new identity to us through such things as money or power. Yet we are already rich in Christ, and we possess power in Him and through the Holy Spirit. One way to kill our kingdom calling, mission, and purpose in life is by dancing to the tune of Satan's fake promises. He promises power, fame, wealth, recognition, and influence only to trap people in his evil schemes and kill their true identity in God.

In God we have all we need. We possess the wealth of heaven and are recognized around the globe because we bear the name of Christ. Nothing can give us greater spiritual wealth or recognition than serving the King of kings and dwelling in His kingdom. As we activate our God-given power and rediscover our identity, however, we must be careful to avoid Satan's seduction. He causes people to desire more power than they already have in Christ or to desire miracles more than the God of wonders and miracles. As noted earlier, God must never be viewed as a vending machine for miracles but as the Holy One who deserves our total worship and desires our fellowship.

Satan's temptation of Eve is recorded in Genesis 3:1-5:

> [The serpent] said to the woman, "Did God really say, 'You can't eat from any tree in the garden'?" The woman said to the serpent, "We may eat the fruit from the trees in the garden. But about the fruit of the tree in the middle of the garden, God said, 'You must not eat it or touch it, or you will die.'" "No! You will not die," the serpent said to the woman. "In fact, God knows that when you eat it your eyes will be opened and you will be like God, knowing good and evil."

Satan's big lie, "You will be like God," sent Adam and Eve into an identity crisis. They forgot who they were and whose they were. They wanted more than what God had already given them. Remember—Adam and Eve were wonderfully and beautifully made in the image of God, and God had given them power over every other creature. They were already like their Father God in many ways because God had created them like Himself. But the big lie and promise from Satan, "You will be like God," caused them to lose their true identity in God and desire a higher position than what God had given them.

In Matthew 4:1–11 the same Satan tempted Jesus three times. He tried to get Jesus to show off His kingdom power by turning stones into bread and throwing Himself down from a lofty peak of the temple and allowing the angels of God to rescue Him. Satan also showed Him all the kingdoms of the world and their splendor and said to Jesus, "I will give You all these things if You will fall down and worship me" (v. 9). But Jesus knew His identity in God and the purpose of the power and authority that had been invested in Him by His Father in heaven, and He powerfully rebuked Satan. He did not fall for his deceptive schemes as Adam and Eve had. Where Adam and Eve failed, Jesus excelled, showing us the way to defeat Satan and all his tactics. Don't fall for Satan's fake promises, because in God and with God you have so much more than Satan could ever offer you. Set your eyes on God and on the kingdom of God, and you shall be lifted and blessed in every area of your life.

One of the primary tactics Satan employs to steal the people's real identity is offering fake power or position. Power in the world is a sought-after commodity because it gives people influence over others. Indeed, some people will do anything to get a position of power in society. However, the greatest power a person can possess is the supernatural power of God. It is a power that sets the captives free and dismantles the demonic forces of this world. It is a power that frees us from the influence of the forces of darkness.

The wars around the world and the disunity we see in the body of Christ are caused mostly by the desire of people for positions of power and control. In the worldly system, power gives an individual control or influence over others, but in the kingdom of God, power is for building up others and setting them free from the influences of the kingdom of darkness. Kingdom power is not for showmanship or self-importance or dominating others. That is why Jesus responded to Satan's temptations as He did. If Jesus wanted to show off His authority and power, He could have easily turned the stones into bread or jumped off the building, knowing the angels would protect Him. But He could not give in to Satan's temptations because He knew who He was—the Son of the almighty God, the creator of the universe and all that is in it.

As Christians, if we want to be powerfully used by God, we need to understand that our gifts or anointing is not what makes us who we are but rather what we have been graciously given to use in proclaiming the good news of the kingdom of God here on earth. The living God who dwells in us makes us who we are. That means that if you don't have the same anointing or gift I have, you don't have to feel less loved by God or less important in His kingdom, because your importance and God's love for you are found not in a particular gift or anointing but in the God who lives and reigns in you. Never allow Satan to steal your identity in God by focusing your life on acquiring a position of power or authority. Again, authority and power are given to us for conducting the business of the kingdom of God here on earth with a gentle spirit and a heart full of grace and compassion for the lost.

If not carefully used, the power of God can easily lead people to think more highly of themselves than they ought to think. This is how Satan kills off our focus and dependence on God for healing and deliverance—he tries to make us think *we* are the ones producing the healing and deliverance. We must emphasize here that while we are powerful in God, power is not our identity. It is simply what we use to bring restoration to those who are bound by the forces of darkness.

It is a great mistake to draw your identity from your position or title in ministry or in the secular world. You can have numerous degrees, money, and a lofty position in the community and yet still be unsatisfied, confused, depressed, and miserable. Those things cannot truly make you happy; they are simply tools or avenues to help you do your work effectively. There is nothing wrong with having lots of money or a title if you can function in it as intended by God, building up and inspiring people for God.

A title simply describes the specific work someone does. It is tragic when people feel worthy in life based on what they do, yet even many Christians have adopted this attitude. Thus, when a position is taken away from them in their church, they leave the church and sometimes even abandon God altogether. We should be able to live for God, proclaim His gospel, and declare His goodness with or without money, ministerial position, or title—that is true dedication and commitment to God.

## With or Without Money or a Title, I Will Still Serve My God

Here is my testimony. When I was serving in my local church as missions director and our pastor decided to eliminate that department, God spoke to me and said, "Will you still serve Me in that same field, winning souls for My kingdom around the globe?" My first and honest answer was "I don't have the resources [money] to do so, a position to function in, and a church to work with and through." The Holy Spirit rebuked me for thinking that way, because it is not money or a position or a local church that enables us to do the work of God—or stops us from doing it. We can begin doing the work of God long before we have all these things because God provides all the resources required to do His work.

The church is there to nurture, motivate, empower, and train us to do what we are called to do for God. So if you have already been trained and equipped in the Word of God, you have no excuse for not doing the work God has called you to. The problem may well be that you see your local church as your only mission field and your fellow believers as souls that need to be rescued. The true mission field, however, is the world, and in the world countless souls urgently need to be rescued. You may need to change your thinking if you are to step out and do the work of God.

The turning point for me was when I accepted and obeyed God's calling on my life and declared to myself, "With or without money, support, or a title, I will still serve my God." Because of that commitment, hundreds of people around the world have been reached with the gospel of Jesus Christ. Don't limit God or what He can do or wants to do through the ordinary you. People may have their own perception of you and tell you who they think you are, but at the end of the day what matters is what God says about you.

When God looks at you, He sees potential, redemption, life, victory, and a mighty man or woman of valor. So don't surrender your kingdom identity or replace it with the names people give you. You may not have money, but that does not mean you are poor. You may have fallen into sin, but that does not mean you are a sinner for life. You may have failed before, but that does not mean you are a failure. No season or circumstance can define who you are—only God can do that. Nobody cannot destroy your identity in God because that identity is ingrained in the very image of God.

One of the great characteristics of God is that He can use any willing soul to do the work of His kingdom, regardless of the person's culture, race, nationality, or education. If you have a willing and humble heart, God will use you and empower you to do exploits for His kingdom whether or not you have an official title or position.

All God looks for is a person with a willing and contrite spirit. So rise up and function both within the body of Christ and outside your local church, using your gifts to help others find Jesus as the way to God the Father.

## The Blood of Jesus Has Restored the Power of God in You

The fall of Adam and Eve did not cause man to lose his identity in God, because man was created in the image of God. Because of sin man lost his ability to function fully in the power of the kingdom of God. Sin disconnects people from the source of their power—God. Nevertheless, through the blood the sinless Son of God, Jesus Christ, spilled on the cross for our sins, God reconnects us back to Himself as His own children when we put our faith in Christ (John 1:12). The remarkable and significant note here is that even after the fall of man, man's identity in God did not change. Although it was marred, it was eventually fixed and restored on the cross through the blood of Jesus Christ, which was shed for the sins of humanity. On the cross Jesus not only redeemed us from the power of sin and death but also recovered and restored the power of the kingdom of God that He had bestowed on His created people in the beginning. We have God's power living in us.

The blood of Jesus Christ has not only redeemed us from the power of the kingdom of darkness and restored our marred identity in God, but it has also restored the power of God in us to do the works of God. Unfortunately, countless Christians don't understand they have the power of God resident in them to do the work of the kingdom of God and to be the victorious overcomers God created them to be. The key is to grasp that our true identity is not in any object but in Christ alone. When we fully embrace this truth, we will discover or rediscover our strength, hope, life, joy, and happiness.

And we will live as Jesus lived, walking in His humble character and in the fullness of God.

Jesus used His kingdom power to set the captives free, not to oppress or look down on the very people He was sent to save. Many people in positions of authority or power make the mistake of using their power to bring down the people they are called to lift up or help. This is because they don't understand who they really are in life. They associate their identity with power and seek to prove their power by oppressing others or putting problems or burdens on people. But in God's design, power is for helping others overcome their problems. This must be understood so that when we begin functioning in the power of the kingdom of God and in His anointing, we will not abuse that power or anointing God has given us. Furthermore, we will not use it for personal gain or for bringing people down but rather for pointing people to Jesus Christ and helping them overcome any obstacles in life that may hinder them from living for God and pursuing His kingdom.

Discovering who we are in Christ, what kind of power and authority God has given us, and why He has given us such power is key to functioning powerfully in our gifts. God has anointed us to be ambassadors of His glorious and powerful kingdom, not for our own gain or prestige but for the advancement of the kingdom of God. By giving mankind authority, power, and dominion over every creature, God did not mean man's identity was to be defined by his dominion. Rather, it was to continue to be defined by the image of the living God in which man was created. This must be emphasized. Authority, power, and dominion are fully given to believers in Christ so they can function in the kingdom of God as kings and priests on behalf of God to bring glory and honor to His name.

## The Purpose of the Power of God in You

The power of God is given for the work of ministry to demonstrate the character of God and to reconnect people to God through healing, deliverance, or miracles. When God uses us to deliver or heal the sick, it doesn't mean our identity becomes that of a healer or deliverer. Jesus alone is the healer and the deliverer, but He has graciously chosen to share His power with us or to manifest His healing and deliverance power through us, His vessels. The moment we begin to think we are the healers is the moment we begin slipping away from fully trusting and depending on God's power to do the supernatural through us. With this thinking come pride and self-elevation to the position of God. God does not share His glory and honor with man, however. It was for this reason Satan was thrown out of heaven like lightning. Our joy as disciples of Jesus Christ comes from having a deep relationship and fellowship with Him, having our names written in the Book of Life, and above all, being the image of God here on earth.

In Luke 10:17–20 Jesus had to remind a group of disciples who had returned from a mission trip He had sent them on about the significance of living for the kingdom of God.

> The seventy-two returned with joy, saying, "Lord, even the demons are subject to us in your name!" And he said to them, "I saw Satan fall like lightning from heaven. Behold, I have given you authority [**reason**] to tread on serpents and scorpions, and over all the power of the enemy, and nothing shall hurt you. Nevertheless [**warning**], do not rejoice in this, that the spirits are subject to you, but [**focus**] rejoice that your names are written in heaven." (ESV)

The power of God moved mightily through the seventy-two disciples, and they were excited about what they had seen and experienced. Indeed, Satan was subject to their authority and power in the name of Jesus Christ. Nevertheless, Jesus had to help them understand the most significant thing to rejoice about in their lives—that their names were written in heaven.

In Matthew 7:21–23 Jesus had this to say:

> Not everyone who says to Me, "Lord, Lord!" will enter the kingdom of heaven, but only the one who does the will of My Father in heaven. On that day many will say to Me, "Lord, Lord didn't we prophesy in Your name, drive out demons in Your name, and do many miracles in Your name?" Then I will announce to them, "I never knew you! Depart from Me, you lawbreakers."

The identity of true disciples of Jesus Christ is found not in how they can prophesy, preach, drive out demons, or perform miracles in the name of Jesus Christ but rather in how they obey the Word of God and live in close fellowship and commitment to Him. When we discover who we are in God and truly understand that He dwells in us, we will learn to fear God more than we fear man, and we will walk in His fullness.

## The Day You Discover Your Identity Is the Day Your Life Begins to Have Meaning

The day I personally discovered who I am in Christ, what He has called me to do for His kingdom, and the power of His kingdom He has made available to me through His grace and through the Holy Spirit, my life and thinking were changed forever. The fear of man, a man-pleasing spirit, the identity crisis, and faithlessness all but disappeared from my life, and my vision and desire in life were narrowed down to pursuing the kingdom of God.

When you are always trying to impress people, your life becomes full of anxiety, stress, fear, and hypocrisy. But when you live to please God and bring honor and glory to His name, you become full of kingdom confidence (not arrogance). You become fearless and determined to pursue God and His Word. Proverbs 29:25 says, "Fear of man will prove to be a snare, but whoever trusts in the Lord is kept safe" (NIV). The day you discover your true identity is the day your life begins to have meaning. The fear of man disappears, replaced by a holy fear of God and desire for the things of God.

As we have noted many times, fear of man can hinder you from functioning in the power of God and discovering your kingdom gifts, calling, and vision. Of course, I am not suggesting that you disobey spiritual leaders God has placed over your life or that you don't honor or respect other people. It is great to have your calling affirmed and confirmed by godly people who have the spirit and vision for expanding the kingdom of God as God commands us. But above all it is God who calls, affirms, and confirms us to do His work. When we talk of avoiding a man-pleasing spirit or the fear of man, we mean to avoid doing the work of God—or any other good deeds—to be loved by people or to gain acceptance from them. The truth is that we can never please people enough to satisfy them because people are always craving more. God is fully satisfied with us, not because of our works but because the righteousness of Christ has been imputed to us by His grace. So doing the work of the kingdom of God doesn't make God love us more than He already does. We do the work of the kingdom of God because God has commanded us to proclaim His good news of freedom to those who are still in captivity. As Jesus has made Himself known to us, so we are to make Him known to others. Sadly, fear and thoughts that we are not good enough or qualified to serve frequently stop us from doing so.

## Your Identity in Christ Qualifies You to Proclaim the Gospel

God wants to use you, not because you are the most qualified, holy, or gifted person on the planet but because His grace specializes in transforming what man has labeled useless or foolish into powerful instruments of the good news of His kingdom to shame the spiritually and religiously wise people of the world. Furthermore, He chooses to work through the despised, lowly, and weak things of the world to shame the strong (see 1 Corinthians 1:26–28). Wherever you may be in life, God wants to transform your life through the power of His Word so He can use you as His instrument of life, hope, peace, and transformation. It's time to stop talking about the need for change in the world and *be* the change the body of Christ and the world need. It's time to stop complaining about all the problems the world, the body of Christ, or your family or marriage are facing and become the solution to those problems through the power of God. Before you were born God chose you and placed in you a spiritual gift and calling so you could represent the affairs of His kingdom on behalf of His people here on earth. You are not just an ordinary person; you are a king and a royal priesthood set apart for the business of the kingdom of heaven. The power to do the will of God rests in discovering and activating the power of the kingdom of God in you. It is through the power of God you can be and do what God originally designed you to be and do and fulfill your potential in life and bless many people.

God wants not only to transform our lives but also to empower every individual with His abilities so the church can rise up and bring restoration to the broken people of God. One of the greatest deceptions the enemy has unleashed on the church is the idea that only a few people are gifted by God and the rest must just sit and do nothing. This is why the church is not doing greater and mightier things in the community of God. Most people are not functioning in their gifts and have not yet realized their kingdom authority. What has killed the work of God in many churches around the world? One individual functioning in the power of God while the rest sit and watch him or her as if they were in a cinema watching their favorite movie star. It's crucial for church leaders and individuals to understand that the move of God cannot be sustained with only a few individual gifts operating. One person or one gift alone cannot overpower the forces of this world. To maintain the fire of God, the entire body of Christ must be functioning as one.

It is true that God often sparks His revival fire through one person (a leader), but that fire must be sustained and maintained by the entire body. The gifts of God are designed not to work separately from one another; they are designed to work in conjunction with one another while they individually produce what they are designed to produce. It's time to learn to serve one another and serve *with* one another. The highly skilled and the lesser skilled must work together to institute the government of God on earth.

Your identity in Christ qualifies you to do what God has called and is calling the church to do. I strongly believe the church will be untouchable and powerful when all the redeemed people of God are ministering both within and outside their local churches. Jeremiah did not know God had already chosen him before he was born to be His voice to the nation of Israel, communicating to them God's instructions. Jeremiah was set apart—withdrawn from living an ordinary (profane) lifestyle—to live an extraordinary lifestyle in the power and protection of the Lord. Jeremiah objected, however. He felt he was not qualified to be used by God.

> [The Lord said,] "Before I formed you in the womb I knew you. And before you were born I consecrated you; I appointed you a prophet to the nations." Then I said, "Ah, Lord God! Behold, I do not know how to speak, for I am only a youth." But the Lord said to me, "Do not say, 'I am only a youth; for to all to whom I send you, you shall go, and whatever I command you, you shall speak. Do not be afraid of them, for I am with you to deliver you, declares the Lord." (Jeremiah 1:5–8 ESV)

One important observation here is that *God does not call the qualified. Rather He qualifies those whom He calls.* He empowers them to bring His kingdom into the hearts of His people here on earth.

**What Does God Say about You?**

Discovering what God says about you can unleash a warrior in you. Just think about how you felt when you discovered people you cherished, respected, and honored were busy gossiping and bad-mouthing you and spreading slander. Your spirit felt crushed, and you were deeply disappointed. The inner you felt like taking them on like a lion taking on an elephant, but the Holy Spirit restrained you, and you forgave them. It is just as impactful when you discover the good things God says about you to the devil and to all his agents. You become a warrior, a mighty man or woman of God, and you can't help but rise up in the power of the Holy Spirit and proclaim the goodness of God and His kingdom to all humanity. Here is how God sees you:

You are a chosen race, a royal priesthood, a holy nation, a people for His possession, so that you may proclaim the praises of the One who called you out of darkness into His marvelous light. Once you were not a people, but now you are God's people. (1 Peter 2:9–10)

Think about that for a second! This overrides all the negative names you have been called by man. When you are struggling with your identity, remember what God says about you:

- You are a child of God (John 1:12).
- You have been justified and redeemed by God (Romans 3:24).
- You are a branch of the true vine and conduit of Christ's life (John 15:1–5).
- You are a friend of the most powerful Man who ever walked on earth—Jesus (John 15:15).
- You are a fellow heir of Christ (Romans 8:17).
- You have been accepted by Christ (Romans 15:7).
- In Christ Jesus you have wisdom, righteousness, sanctification, and redemption (1 Corinthians 1:30).
- You are a new creature (2 Corinthians 5:17).
- You have been set free in Christ (Galatians 5:1).
- You are a member of Christ's body and a partaker of His promises (Ephesians 3:6).
- You have boldness and confident access to God through faith in Christ (Ephesians 3:12).
- You are a citizen of heaven, not earth (Philippians 3:20).
- The peace of God guards your heart and mind (Philippians 4:7).

And the list goes on and on.

As I travel around the world preaching the gospel of our Lord Jesus Christ, it is heartbreaking to see so many Christians who don't know who they are in Christ—what they have in Him and what He has called them to do both individually and corporately. God has not called us to just sit and do nothing. He has called us to do His kingdom work, and He is waiting on us to become channels through whom He can touch the nations and spark a kingdom fire in the hearts of people around the world.

This is the time to discover, recover, and reignite the power of God that is in you so together with the rest of the body of Christ you can forcefully advance the kingdom of God. Furthermore, as you obey the voice and Word of God, He will rejuvenate the power of the Holy Spirit in you and activate the anointing of God on your life so you can demonstrate the glory of God.

# Chapter 10

# IT'S TIME TO RISE UP

God Is with You—Fear Not

In Matthew 25 Jesus taught His disciples a profound lesson in the parable of the talents.

> For it is just like a man going on a journey. He called his own slaves and turned over his possessions to them. To one he gave five talents; to another, two; and to another, one-to each according to his own ability. Then he went on a journey. Immediately the man who had received five talents went, put them to work, and earned five more. In the same way the man with two earned two more. But the man who had received one talent went off, dug a hole in the ground, and hid his master's money. After a long time the master of those slaves came and settled accounts with them. The man who had received five talents approached, presented five more talents, and said, "Master, you gave me five talents. Look, I've earned five more talents." His master said to him, "Well done, good and faithful slave! You were faithful over a few things; I will put you in charge

of many things. Share your master's joy!" Then the man with two talents also approached. He said, "Master, you gave me two talents. Look, I've earned two more talents." His master said to him, "Well done, good and faithful slave! You were faithful over a few things; I will put you in charge of many things. Share your master's joy!" Then the man who had received one talent also approached and said, "Master, I know you. You're a difficult man, reaping where you haven't sown and gathering where you haven't scattered seed. So I was afraid and went off and hid your talent in the ground. Look, you have what is yours." But his master replied to him, "You evil, lazy slave! If you knew that I reap where I haven't sown and gather where I haven't scattered, then you should have deposited my money with the bankers. And when I returned I would have received my money back with interest. So take the talent from him and give it to the one who has 10 talents. For to everyone who has, more will be given, and he will have more than enough. But from the one who does not have, even what he has will be taken away from him." (Matthew 25:14–29)

## What Do We Learn from This Important Parable?

The main character in this parable is the master who distributed talents to his servants before he went on a long journey. The master in the parable symbolizes Jesus, and his long journey points to the lengthy delay that precedes Jesus' second coming. The servants, or slaves, represent believers in Christ. The talents represent the gifts Jesus entrusts to us according to our abilities so we can serve in

His kingdom and reproduce those gifts. All believers, regardless of religious or cultural background, have been given the privilege and opportunity to serve in the kingdom of God through gifts God has invested in them.

The faithful and fearless servants in Jesus' parable used the gifts and resources given to them to reproduce more. The fearful slave went out and hid his gift because he had a wrong perception of his master. He misjudged the master to be a difficult man, reaping where he did not sow seed and gathering where he had not scattered seed.

**What Is in Your Hand?**

As followers of Christ we cannot say we have no talent or gift. God has gifted every one of His children. The problem is that many of us have hidden our gifts because of fear or because we are not content with the gifts we have. Jesus' parable makes it clear that God will not entrust us with more opportunities and blessings if we do not use what we already have to serve Him and produce spiritual fruit. We ask God to give us more, and yet God has already given us all the resources we need to succeed in what He has called us to do.

If we don't tap into the resources God has already given us, we will continue doing nothing and producing nothing, while others thrive and excel at what they do. You may be asking right now, "What is my gift?" The Lord's response to that question is another question: "What is in your hand?"

When God called Moses to go and rescue the Israelites from Egypt, Moses had some doubts. He felt he had no resources or abilities God could use. He also did not think the people would believe him.

Moses answered, "What if they won't believe me and will not obey me but say, 'The Lord did not appear to you'?" The Lord asked him,

"What is that in your hand?" "A staff," Moses replied. The God said, "Throw it on the ground." He threw it on the ground, and it became a snake. Moses ran from it, but the Lord told him, stretch out your hand and grab it by the tail." So he stretched out his hand and caught it, and it became a staff in his hand. "This will take place [signs and wonders], He continued, "so they will believe that the Lord, the God of their fathers, the God of Abraham, the God of Isaac, and the God of Jacob, has appeared to you." (Exodus 4:1–5)

What was God telling Moses here, and what does His message reveal to us today? The Lord was telling Moses that He would use what Moses already had in his hand to show the people He had sent him to rescue them. And here is what God is saying to us today: He will use whatever is already in our hand, whether it is a hundred dollars, a gift of hospitality, or any other resource.

Whatever you have and wherever you are in life, God can use that to take you to a higher place in Him where you can do greater things. Don't despise who you are or what you have, and don't let other people despise who you are or what you have. Through you God can touch a city or a nation. Just get over your fears, and see God use you tremendously for His glory. You don't have to be extremely smart, gifted, or rich or belong to a certain elite club to be used by God. God can use anyone, regardless of his or her ethnicity, nationality, wealth or poverty, knowledge, or gift. Therefore, you have no excuse for not rising up and using what God has blessed you with to be a blessing to other people and a channel through whom millions can experience God's grace, mercy, life, and hope.

## Keys to Fulfilling Your Kingdom Calling

The keys to fulfilling your kingdom assignment and functioning productively in your gift are listed here:

- Discovering your kingdom power and authority
- Discovering your identity in Christ
- Obeying God and His voice, even in the face of adversity, animosity, or rejection
- Returning to God if you have strayed from His presence
- Standing on the Word of God and not on the words of man
- Following selfless, godly examples who will encourage you and hold you accountable

While we have discussed each of these points already—some at great length—it is helpful to review them briefly to see how they all fit together in your life.

> Without knowing who you are in Christ and or what kind of power you have in God, it is impossible to step out in faith and do what God has called you to do for Him. For instance, if you know God with all your heart, soul, and mind and you know the power you have in Him, obeying Him will be natural. When His voice says, "Go and declare the good news of the kingdom to people of all nations," there will be a fire burning deep in your soul so you can only say to yourself, "Woe is me if I do not preach the gospel!" (1 Corinthians 9:16).

Returning to God is another key to fulfilling God's mission and purpose. We cannot do anything great in life without being in God and walking with Him. In the Bible we see that each time the nation of Israel strayed from the presence of God, they suffered disaster and defeat (Leviticus 26:17). However, whenever they returned to God with repentant hearts and worshipped Him alone and called on His name, God heard their prayers in heaven, forgave their sins, and gave them victory over their enemies. Obedience brings God's blessings (Deuteronomy 28:1–14), while disobedience brings a curse or defeat in life (Deuteronomy 28:15–68). It is important to clearly understand that the number-one key to fulfilling our potential in life is returning to our God and living our lives according to His Word and upholding His Word in our hearts. This doesn't mean we will do this perfectly, but it does mean we have decided to follow God no matter what may come our way. If we fail, we must repent and rise up and continue marching on with our God, because nothing can or should separate us from His love for us and from the mission He has called us to.

Another important key that will help us fulfill our calling in life is standing on the Word of God as an anchor of our faith in God. God's Word is our blueprint for living out the fullness of His purpose for His glory. Without walking in the power of the Word of God, we cannot live life to our maximum potential or fulfill our kingdom call. We can never do great and mighty things in life without Jesus and His Word at the center of our hearts. We need God's Word every day of our life, and we must walk in it if are to be what God originally created us to be. As we walk in the power of God's Word, He will be with us and empower us to live for Him and advance His kingdom here on earth.

Also, we must understand that we cannot fulfill the call of God on our lives without the help and encouragement of other people. The Bible says, "As iron sharpens iron, so one person sharpens another" (Proverbs 27:17). We need to find friends who can sharpen and encourage us to pursue God and do His will, not so-called friends who constantly discourage us or look down on us. Having great friends who have a kingdom mind-set and the heart of God will help us grow and mature spiritually and develop a spirit of humility. As Christians, we need one another. We need to serve under the leadership of kingdom-focused men and women of God who hear the voice of God and earnestly desire to develop other people for the service of God.

I can personally testify that I am who I am today in the kingdom of God simply because of other men and women of God under whom I served after giving my life to the Lord. Serving under these men and women of God empowered me to do the work of ministry effectively, and their support and prayers all these years have greatly encouraged me.

When I was a young man and minister living in Zambia, Africa, a great man of God helped me grow spiritually. He gave me opportunities to develop my gift of evangelism through hands-on ministry. Along with other young men from our church, I would go to this man of God's house every Saturday. His wife would make us breakfast, and then he would send us out into the community to evangelize and preach the gospel to people. We went door to door, asking at each home if there was any sick person in the house. If so, we would pray for that one, and God would instantly heal the person. Many people we ministered to gave their lives to Jesus Christ.

As youths we needed such a servant of God in our lives who would send us out in faith to proclaim the gospel of Jesus Christ, while at the same time providing spiritual covering for us as we did the work of evangelism. It was through these experiences in 2002 that I discovered God's calling on my life to be an evangelist to the nations.

We all need godly people in our life who are secure in the Lord and comfortable enough in His presence and in their giftings that they are not afraid to develop, motivate, inspire, and raise up other people to serve in the kingdom of God. Make sure you sit under a godly leader who will mentor you and provide spiritual covering. Don't go out there all by yourself just because God has called you or because you have a gift. Satan likes to attack and bring down loners. Spiritual covering is extremely important, for we are accountable both to God and to one another.

Despite all the self-centeredness and competitiveness we see in the Christian world today, there are still many men and women of God dedicated to raising up a new generation of leaders in the world without manipulating them or seeking praise for themselves, men and women who have the spirit and heart of Jesus Christ—selfless and kingdom focused. With such leaders in your life, you will flourish in the Lord and do exploits for His kingdom. When you are so kingdom focused, you can flourish and be a blessing to the body of Christ in any spiritual environment or ministry.

Obeying God is one of the greatest keys to fulfilling your kingdom call and overcoming every voice that brings discouragement, doubt, or fear into your heart. Obeying God and being faithful to worship and glorifying His holy name are crucial to fulfilling your destiny in life. When you obey God's Word and uphold it in your heart, there is nothing God cannot do for you and through you. Obedience is better than sacrifice (1 Samuel 15:22), but it comes at a price. You may lose some friends or be rejected when you obey God's call on your life and begin to walk in it. You may be ignored, mocked, or attacked by jealous and self-serving people. However, when you obey God at the expense of your reputation, God will reward you in ways you cannot even fathom and surprise your enemies by constantly providing for you and expanding your influence to the glory and honor of His awesome name.

As you trust and follow Jesus Christ, He will use you mightily to bring healing and transformation. You must keep your eyes on Him, be teachable and humble, and let even the difficult experiences in your life prepare you to step out into the world and do the work of God without being shaken or fearful. Pride can destroy God's vision for your life, so walk in humility, forgiving those who may have wronged you and honoring those who may have rejected you so God can manifest His glory through you.

## When God Calls You, Others Do Not Get the Memo

When you are just starting out in life, there may be few who want to associate with you, but when you endure and God blesses you, everybody wants to associate with you and be your friend and work with you. Why? People can see only what is immediately in front of them, and their decisions are usually based on shortsighted concerns. Sadly, many, if not most, Christians are no different.

Our God is the only One who sees beyond what is right in front of us. He forgives us and loves us while we are nobodies yet in sin. He does not call the qualified but sanctifies those He calls and qualifies them to do His kingdom duties. It is fascinating that when God calls people to serve Him, He doesn't send out a memo to let everyone know about it. People will find out you have been called or gifted by God only when you step out and do what you are called to do. If you are waiting for someone other than God to affirm your calling or encourage you or support you right from the start, then you will miss your destiny in life and live in disappointment. It is God who calls you to serve Him, so He is your encourager, supporter, and source of strength. He will bring key people into your life to uplift you, pray for you, encourage you, and support you—and sometimes they are people you would never think would help you fulfill the calling of God on your life.

When you focus on God and seek His kingdom only, He will be there to strengthen you and make a way for you when you are going through challenges. Above all, you must encourage yourself through the power of the Word of God, just as David found strength in the Lord his God when he was going through challenges (1 Samuel 30:6). The Word of God can bring strength, courage, and determination into our lives in any circumstance. People may not recognize your call and some may question your gifting, but that should not be a reason for you to sit and do nothing in life or to fail to rise up and use your gift. When Yahweh calls you, others do not get a memo. Always remember this when you are opposed and discouraged and feel like giving up.

Your time to stand up and begin to do the work of God and use your gift is *now*. Rise up and wake up in the Spirit of God, and let your heart be governed by the government of the kingdom of God. May the Lord Jesus Christ ignite your gift and passion to serve Him and revive your spirit and cause you to do what He has called you to do for the benefit of the body of Christ. May all your fears, anger, bitterness, and disappointments be flushed out of your life. May courage, boldness, and determination rise within you as you rise up to advance the kingdom of God.

**Together Let Us Rise Up!**

We who are spiritual leaders must never feel insecure about raising up other leaders or raising up our spiritual sons and daughters into fully grown spiritual leaders and giving them opportunities to raise up other leaders and disciples for Jesus Christ. We must do our best to train all who are willing and to allow the Holy Spirit to facilitate their spiritual growth so they join us as together we advance the kingdom of God.

Jesus was extremely interested in raising up leaders who would carry on the work of His Father's kingdom until His second coming. He appointed His disciples and trained them for a bigger assignment. In John 14:12 He made a powerful statement that revealed the true heart of God: "I assure you: The one who believes in Me will also do the works that I do. And he will do even greater works than these, because I am going to the Father." Any leader who has never raised up another leader and allowed that one to freely do the work of God without manipulation is not a true leader from God.

God wants us, His children, to function in unity in the body of Christ and do greater works by carrying His good news into the whole world, using every spiritual gift He has graciously gifted to the church. Imagine all Christians selflessly functioning in their God-given gifts in the body of Christ today. The church would be a force to reckon with, and the power of the Holy Spirit would set nations around the world on fire. Together we the church are unstoppable, and the enemy has no power over us because five of us can chase a hundred, and a hundred of us can chase and destroy ten thousand of Satan's agents (Leviticus 26:8). But for us to see this happen, each one of us must rise to the occasion, because an army or team is only as good and effective as its individual soldiers or players. Our commander in chief, God, is waiting on all of us to take up our places and do His work in unity and not with a spirit of competition. In the kingdom of God there is nothing to compete for because everyone has a share. Competition is not of God; it is of the devil. We are to work in unity, supporting one another in every way possible so the gospel can reach as many people as possible around the world.

The church cannot usher in the government of the kingdom of God here on earth through only a few leaders. It takes the entire army of the Lord. We tend to forget this and consequently despise and exclude certain people and their gifts. Everyone in the kingdom of God is vital to God's mission to the nations, and no one soldier can win a spiritual battle single-handedly. He or she needs other soldiers with different skill sets to accomplish the mission. This is why God is calling *all* of us to rise up and work as one body. When we rise, He will arise with us and through us do mighty things in the world. We should never think we are the only ones God wants to work through to change the world. No, He wants to move in the entire body of Christ to bring healing to this sick and desperately wicked world.

We need to develop a culture of unity, honor, respect, and love for one another and for one another's gifts, callings, and ministries so we can function in unity and as one body. And above all, we need to develop a culture of honoring God. It's time for the church to arise and empower every man and woman, young and old, to do the work of God.

It is sad to say, but the church for the most part has been fighting one another for many years instead of focusing on the real enemy, Satan, and his influence on the world in which we live. We fight over things like who has the best worship team or band, the best gift, greatest talent, biggest church, or nicest building instead of uniting to fight the devil as he tries to destroy God's people. We have been fighting the wrong battles at the expense of those who are perishing or being tormented by evil spirits through sickness and diseases. We fight over people, split up over small things, and push people away from our churches because of our super-spiritual attitudes. Instead of guiding, nurturing, and helping people to grow in their gifts, we criticize them or call them names and bring them down—that is the spirit of witchcraft and Satan. As a result, we have unwittingly created a dysfunctional and powerless "Christianity" that cannot help or serve those who are dying spiritually.

We have even created a humanistic religion focused on praising and worshipping man rather than God. We fear man more than we fear the God who created us and sees everything under the sun. We do things to please man so he can give us important positions or praise instead of doing things to bring honor and glory to the name of God. I don't mean we should not honor people; I mean our ministry services should be done unto God and not unto man. It is time to move away from a man-pleasing Christianity and begin to praise and glorify God in all we do.

The reason God wants us to rise up and use our gifts is not so we can be superstars or look important in the eyes of man but so we can function here on earth according to His kingdom purpose and plan for setting the captives free, mending and restoring the brokenhearted, and making God's nature known to all people groups. Whenever we find people doing the work of God and preaching sound doctrine, we should compliment and encourage them to keep doing the work of God. To reach all people with the gospel of our Lord Jesus Christ, we need to mobilize the church with people of various gifts and from all nations and tribes of the earth.

## We All Belong to the Same Team—Team Jesus

In Mark 9:38–40, we read this:

> John said to [Jesus], "Teacher, we saw someone casting out demons in Your name, and we tried to prevent him because he was not following us." But Jesus said, "Do not hinder him, for there is no one who will perform a miracle in My name, and be able soon afterward to speak evil of me. For he who is not against us is for us." (NASB)

It is ironic the disciples told the man they found casting out demons in the name of Jesus Christ to stop simply because he was not in their group or following them. The disciples' attitude showed that they thought they were the only ones authorized and qualified to use the name of Jesus Christ and to cast out demons in His name. It is interesting that these same disciples had failed to cast out a demon earlier (Mark 9:14–29), and yet they had the audacity to stop someone who was actually successful in doing so! Sadly, this same attitude is common today in the body of Christ. When some Christians see others doing the work of God in their community or neighborhood, they begin to attack their character or credibility and question their qualifications or call. They tell everyone to stay away from such people. Instead of developing a working relationship with other people of God, they quickly establish an adversarial relationship with them, as if they belong to or work for a different Jesus.

Jesus did not come to work with only a few or to rescue or empower only certain people. Neither did He die for only a few people. He came to rescue and empower every person who would believe in Him and accept the influence of His rule and reign. Furthermore, He paid for the sins of all, not just a few people. Consequently, He wants to use *all* of us to demonstrate His rule and reign to the nations. We must not stop or hinder others from preaching the gospel if they are sound in doctrine, for such people are not against us or against God—they are for us and with us. We must be secure enough in our gifts and talents, as well as in God, that we don't feel intimidated or jealous when God uses other people mightily in ways He does not use us. Instead, we must complement and support one another as we all do the work of our Father in heaven. Your gift and call of God is as important as other people's gifts and callings, and you must always remember that.

Why are we not seeing the power of God move among us Christians? Why do we not see God doing powerful things in the nations or in our communities? The answer is very simple: God's people are not functioning in the power of the gifts God has given them. Instead, they are following the traditions and religious ways of man. Accordingly, teachers instruct people in the Word of God so they will know what the Word of God says, but they discourage and oppose anyone who actually steps out and does what the Word commands. They teach people to go into the nations and preach the gospel, but when people respond to that teaching and start sharing the gospel in their communities according to their gifts, they are labeled rebellious, disobedient, and full of themselves because in reality the teachers think they are the only ones who can do the work. This spirit in the body of Christ has caused churches to split or become dysfunctional at all levels. Instead of working in the unity of the gifts God has graciously deposited in each of us, we work in disunity, making the church powerless and without impact upon our communities.

The Bible does not instruct us to preach the Word of God to make people happy or to simply let them know what it says. Rather, it instructs us to teach the Word to equip God's people to do the work of ministry and build up the body of Christ. Jesus chose and equipped His disciples for the work of His Father's kingdom, not so they would be amazed by His anointed teaching. He wanted His teaching to consume them, motivate them, and empower them.

If every man and woman, young and old, can be equipped with the Word of God and allowed to function in it with support and love, we, like the Christians in the book of Acts, are going to see the manifest presence of God saturate the world we live in and transform it. The world is perishing in sin, and yet the people who have the cure for the spiritual diseases taking over the world have locked themselves up inside the four walls of the church. It is time for the church to awaken from its sleep and begin to function here on earth as the light of God, demonstrating the power of God's kingdom. But for this to happen, every person must put his or her gifts to use. Whatever gift God has blessed you with, you must function in it with humility and in unity with other men and women of God.

We are gifted and anointed to build up, or edify, the body of Christ, but until we walk in the power of our gifts and function in them, the church will continue to be a sleeping giant. The moment all believers in Christ start using their gifts, the activities of the kingdom of God will increase and bring healing, restoration, and deliverance. Now is the time for the church to rise and shine and demonstrate the power of the kingdom of God. It is time to discover or rediscover the power of the kingdom of God that is in every believer in Christ. If we do not use all the gifts God has given to His church, the people we are called to help or rescue will suffer.

As I travel around the world ministering in different churches, some pastors say to me, "We can't go out to evangelize because we don't have an evangelist in our church." My response is, "You have a lot of evangelists in your church. You just haven't recognized them or given them an opportunity because they don't look like evangelists to you."

In every congregation God has placed all the gifts that church needs to function effectively. In many cases, however, church leaders stand in the way of activating these gifts because of their preferences or their pride. Ephesians 4:11 tells us that Jesus gave to the church apostles, prophets, evangelists, pastors, and teachers to equip the saints for the work of ministry and to build up His body. This means that for the church to fulfill its purpose, all these gifts must work in unity as one body and not separate. Unfortunately, today most of the above-mentioned gifts work in isolation from one another. Consequently, we don't see the full manifest power of God in operation. We have settled for less. It is crucial to understand that we can't go on like this if we truly want to see the fullness of the power and presence of God at work in our midst. The kingdom of God is not about individualism; it is about a corporate and united body with all the parts of the body functioning according to their purpose and design.

Every individual in the kingdom of God has a duty, a purpose, and a calling on his or her life. We understand that not all are called into leadership or to be pastors, evangelists, apostles, or teachers, but the Holy Spirit has graciously given each individual some kingdom ability to bring edification to the body of Christ. The church is a church simply because of the people who assemble in it. Without people the church is nothing but an empty building. God is not interested in the building we call a church but in the people who assemble in it. Therefore, His focus is on equipping every saint to do the work of ministry and to build up other parts of the body of Christ so they can do the same work.

You may think you have no gift to offer to the body of Christ because you are not a pastor, evangelist, teacher, prophet, or apostle, but the best gift you can offer to God is yourself. God does not work only through people with a title; He works through available individuals who say yes to His call. Remember: God is the one who qualifies the unqualified, and He calls people according to His plan and purpose. So never should you feel insignificant or useless. People may tell you that you are useless, but to God you are useful. All you need is to discover the power of His kingdom.

## Summary and Conclusion

### A Brief Summary

Why do we need to discover the power of God within us? Without the power of the kingdom of God working in and through us, it is impossible to do any of this:

- Advance the kingdom of God here on earth
- Overcome the schemes of the kingdom of darkness
- Rescue or set free those who are still in bondage to the forces of darkness
- Influence people for Jesus Christ with the good news of the kingdom

- Demonstrate the true character and nature of God and His kingdom to the nations
- Unleash the rule and reign of God in dark places
- Walk and work in unity with other believers in Christ as one body
- Walk in love, forgiveness, and peace with other people
- Walk in authority, power, and dominion over the forces of darkness
- Heal the sick and win souls for the kingdom of God
- Live a fruitful and prosperous life in Christ
- Win life's spiritual battles

God did not create us to do nothing for His kingdom. We are saved from the kingdom of darkness and brought into the kingdom of light to serve God and to save many others from the kingdom of darkness. We are gifted and anointed to represent the kingdom of God in power and in the fullness of God's glory. I believe when we learn how to allow the reign of God to take charge of our spirits, minds, and souls, we can do great works for the kingdom of God and declare the Word of God and testify of His mercy, grace, and goodness to the world. God's desire and plan for each one of us believers in Christ is to clothe us with His power and abilities so we can soundly do the work of His kingdom.

Far too long believers in Christ have sat in churches and enjoyed the Word of God and the presence of God but have failed to take God's message outside the church to influence lives for Jesus Christ. When we are not doing what we are called to do or be in life, we become easily demoralized and uninterested in the work of God. It's time to break away from the culture and mentality of doing nothing and begin to use the Word of God to bring much-needed restoration and spiritual awakening to the world.

When God truly reigns in you and me, it is impossible for us to remain seated and silent in our comfort zones without responding to His call to be His witnesses to the nations. God created us to function in His kingdom, not to just sit idle and warm the pews. He gave us the power not only to be His sons and daughters but also to set free those captive to sin, sickness, and spiritual blindness. Every congregant must be helped to find his or her place in the local assembly, not by force but by a gentle, heartfelt explanation of the vision of that assembly.

# CONCLUSION

God gave us gifts and different spiritual offices or ministry gifts so when all the gifts are functioning in unity, restoration and reformation will pour out nonstop like rain over the nations. Leviticus 26:8 has this to say about what happens when all the army of the Lord work together in unity to achieve the kingdom goal or agenda: "Five of you will chase a hundred, and a hundred of you will chase ten thousand, and your enemies will fall before you by the sword." This scripture points us to the supernatural victories over the kingdom of darkness God gives His people when they join hands and allow the reign of the Holy Spirit to capture their hearts and fight for the kingdom of God as one. For this reason I am convinced that God today wants to raise up you and me as part of His army so His Spirit and power can rule and reign first in us as individuals and then through us as a corporate body.

For the corporate body to function powerfully, each individual who is part of that body must flow with the power of the Holy Spirit and operate in his or her ministry gift. We should never forget that the corporate body is only as strong, stable, and powerful as the individuals who make up that body. But we also must emphasize that for the individual to stand strong in faith and in the Lord and do the work of God, he or she needs the corporate body, because together we are unbeatable. The individual needs the corporate body as much as the corporate body needs the individual. If the church can grasp this truth, we will without doubt do exploits for the kingdom of God and focus on training and equipping men and women, young and old, for the continuing work of ministry as disciples of Jesus Christ and not of man.

As a Christian you must understand that God has given you His Spirit, His power, His Word, and His authority to run your spiritual race successfully. In 2 Timothy 4:7, near the end of his life, Paul wrote these life-defining words: "I have fought the good fight, I have finished my race, and I have remained faithful." Through the power of God within you, you too can fight a good fight of faith and finish the race.

But remember: no one can run your spiritual race for you. You alone are responsible to train your mind, soul, and body with the Word of God so you can run to win. You run the spiritual race by living for God, serving His kingdom, and serving others. This is the will of God for your life. Sharing about the goodness, mercy, grace, and power of the kingdom of God is one of the greatest races you can ever run. Running a kingdom race doesn't mean being perfect, but it does mean your faith is in Jesus Christ, who ran the race for you already and purchased the victory for you.

Running a kingdom race is all about obedience to the Word of God and the humility to execute what God commands us to do through His Word—to proclaim the good news of His kingdom to all people of all nations. Only people who know how to allow the rule and reign of God to actively operate in and through them can effectively proclaim the Word of God. Too many of us Christians have been taught the Word of God, but when it comes to functioning in its power, we struggle because we have been trained to know and not to do. If we are to see the power of God move in the nations, we need to change our mentality and step out in faith and courage, for "God has not given us a spirit of fear, but of power and of love and of a sound mind" (2 Timothy 1:7 NKJV) so we can do the will of our Father in heaven.

When God reigns in you, you can't remain silent. You have discovered you have the power of God in you through Jesus Christ and through the Holy Spirit, so now rise up and function in the power of your gifts. Awaken the fire of God in you so you can overcome any adversity, because before you reach your destiny, you will face obstacles. In those difficult times, stand still and hear the voice of God. Don't panic in a crisis, because you know who you are in God. It is time to rise up and shine with the glory and power of God. God is waiting on you. Now rise up in His power, and do what you have been anointed to do, for God is with you. Amen!

# 30 INSPIRATIONAL QUOTES TO FEED YOUR SPIRIT

1. God has made us kings and priests, not for decorative purposes or so we can feel good about ourselves but for the demonstration of His kingship.
2. Inside you reside the fire of the Holy Spirit and the light of the glory of God, which needs to burn more brightly to the world so people can see Jesus in you and through you.
3. There isn't anything humble about not doing what God has commissioned you to do. To set aside God's will to appease others is false humility.
4. Humility is responding to the Word of God by doing what it says you are to do out of love for God and people and with consideration for others.
5. Sitting and doing nothing or saying nothing isn't humility at all; it's a destroyer of your destiny.
6. If you don't fight for your destiny, no one will fight for you.
7. When you know what you want in life and know that the God of all power and strength is with you, no criticism, opposition, or negative words can stop you.
8. As long as your intention is to bring glory to the name of God, help others, and build up the body of Christ, you should never be discouraged by any storms of life that come in the form of criticism, resistance, rejection, and hostility.

You must fight all those things to reach your destiny and fulfill your call in life.
9. Show me a person who has never failed in life, and I will show you a person who is scared to try anything new in life.
10. Courage does not come by listening to negative, fearful, and timid people.
11. Your testimony is crucial because it tells the enemy God is powerful enough to turn your mess into a message, your test into a testimony, and your tribulations into a great triumph.
12. When you are going through the challenges of life, don't see yourself as a victim or a failure; see yourself as God sees you—a victor.
13. Your testimony is powerful, and it can help you have courage in the face of adversity because it reminds you of the miraculous deeds of God and His matchless strength and power.
14. Our God is full of power, and His eyes are like a blazing fire (Revelation 1:14; 2:18), so why fear man or Satan? If God is with you, who can be against you or stop you from carrying out His purposes (Romans 8:31)?
15. No one is stopping you from becoming what God created you to be, and no one but yourself is stopping you from using your gift.
16. It's only through the Word of God and sound doctrine that we can revive our faith in God and connect to His power.
17. Knowing how to connect to the power of God during adversity is critically important. Being "religious" alone cannot help you in difficult times. You have to know God and connect your heart, soul, mind, spirit, and body to Him through fellowship, prayer, worship, praise, and your testimony of Him.
18. When you are in a storm, remember God's plans for your life and what His Word says concerning you and all His

promises to you, and let that be the anchor of your soul and of your faith in God.
19. Not knowing who you are in God and what you can do through Him can make you a "fake," a person who seeks attention, tries to please others, and is easily manipulated by people.
20. We make a grave mistake trying to find our identity through people or through our careers, titles, or gifts. Our identity cannot be found in any of those things; it can be found only in God, our Creator.
21. When you know who you are in God, you won't compromise the calling of God on your life just to gain man's approval or to gain wealth or popularity, because it doesn't profit a person to gain the whole world and forfeit his soul (Mark 8:36).
22. One way to kill our kingdom calling, mission, and purpose in life is by dancing to the tune and music of Satan's fake promises. He promises power, fame, wealth, recognition, and influence only to trap people in his evil schemes and kill their true identity in God.
23. Don't fall for Satan's fake promises, because in God and with God you have all that He tries to offer you. Set your eyes on God and on the kingdom of God, and you shall be lifted up and blessed in every area of your life.
24. Kingdom power is not for showmanship or self-importance or dominating others.
25. You should be able to live for God, proclaim His gospel, and declare His goodness with or without money, ministerial position, or title—that is true dedication and commitment to Him.
26. People may have their own perception of you and tell you who they think you are, but at the end of the day what matters is what God says about you and not what people say you are.

27. One of the great characteristics of God is that He can use any willing soul to do the work of His kingdom, regardless of the person's culture, race, nationality, or education.
28. Jesus used His kingdom power to set the captives free, not to oppress or look down upon the very people He was sent to save.
29. God wants to use you, not because you are the most qualified, holy, or gifted person on the planet but because His grace specializes in transforming what man has labeled useless or foolish into powerful instruments of the good news of His kingdom in order to shame the spiritually and religiously wise people of the world.
30. This is your season and time to rise above every setback and challenge and become all God destined you to be. Let the Holy Spirit rule and reign in you, and you will live a successful and fruitful life in the Lord. With God's power you can do and be all He has called you to do and be and thrive in His presence.

# ABOUT THE AUTHOR

Evangelist Dr. Kazumba Charles is a Zambian-born Canadian. He is a powerful Bible teacher, conference speaker, and television and radio host of *Kingdom Insight*. He is founder and director of Christ Passion Evangelistic Ministries. His ministry works with pastors and local churches around the world in training and equipping men and women of God for passionate evangelistic work and local outreaches and sparks the fire of God in the hearts and lives of believers in Christ.

Dr. Kazumba ministers in many nations around the world through crusades, leadership seminars, and conferences. Through his ministry thousands have given their lives to Jesus Christ and hundreds have experienced the power and presence of God in Canada, the United States, India, Zambia, South Africa, Lesotho, Botswana, Uganda, Tanzania, Kenya, Malawi, Rwanda, Burundi, the Democratic Republic of Congo, and elsewhere. God has gifted Dr. Charles with a unique ability and anointing to preach the gospel of Jesus Christ and to teach the Word of God with a demonstration of God's power, presence, and passion in the fullness of the Holy Spirit, bringing life, hope, restoration, and revival into the lives of countless people around the world.

God has also gifted Dr. Kazumba with an ability to reach diverse groups of people with the power of the Word of God. His burning desire is to reach millions of people for Jesus Christ and to empower and develop a new generation of anointed, passionate, loving, caring, and devoted men and women of God. Join hands with this passionate yet humble man of God to win souls for Jesus Christ and advance the kingdom of God to the ends of the earth.

For more information about the ministry of Dr. Kazumba Charles and other books he has written, please visit www.kazumbacharles.com and www.christpassion.org.